LETTERPRESS PRINTING

When any of the workmen
affirm anything that is not
believed, the compositor
knocks with the back corner
of his composing stick against
the lower ledge of his lower
case, and the pressman knocks
the handles of his ball-stocks
together, thereby signifying
the discredit they give to
this story.

JOSEPH MOXON
Mechanick Exercises on the
Whole Art of Printing
1683–1684

Letterpress Printing

A manual for modern fine press printers

Paul Maravelas

OAK KNOLL PRESS
THE BRITISH LIBRARY

First published by
Oak Knoll Press in 2005
310 Delaware Street, New Castle, Delaware 19720 USA
web: http://www.oakknoll.com
and
The British Library
96 Euston Road, London, NW1 2DB, UK

ISBN: 0-7123-4912-X (The British Library)
ISBN: 1-58456-167-X (Oak Knoll Press)
ISBN: 1-58456-174-2 (Oak Knoll Press pb)

Title: Letterpress Printing
       A Manual for Modern Fine Press Printers
Author: Paul Maravelas
Typographer: Will Powers
Illustrator: Paul Maravelas
Jacket photographer: Bruce Challgren
Publishing Director: J. Lewis von Hoelle

*The British CIP Record for this book is available
from the British Library, London, UK*

*Library of Congress
Cataloging-in-Publication Data*
Maravelas, Paul, 1956–
     Letterpress printing / by Paul Maravelas.
        p.   cm.
     Includes bibliographic references and index.
     ISBN 1-58456-167-X   ISBN: 1-58456-174-2 (pb)
     1. Letterpress printing.   I. Title
     Z244.M32 2005
     686.2′312—dc22   2005050860

This work was printed and bound in the United States of America on archival, acid-free paper meeting the requirements of the American Standard for Permanence of paper for Printed Library Materials.

Contents

List of Figures

Acknowledgements

I am grateful to all of the mentors and printers who welcomed me into their craft over the last decades, as I am grateful to the many people who shared advice and information in the writing of this book.

Three printers read a draft of this work and contributed comments: Mike Coughlin, of Cornucopia, Wisconsin; Chip Schilling, of Minneapolis; and Harold E. Sterne, of Sarasota, Florida. Harold Sterne, who spent part of his career training printers at a technical college, and another part of his career researching the history of printing, provided a continuous supply of technical material and advice.

Richard Hopkins of Terra Alta, West Virginia, well known for his role in preserving the craft of typecasting, read and commented on the section relating to type and typecasting.

My wife, Joni Scheftel, D.V.M., M.P.H., an epidemiologist at the Minnesota Department of Health, wrote the sections on the health effects of lead and solvents. Erik Zabel, PH.D., M.P.H., also of the Minnesota Department of Health, shared technical information for the section on lead. A local who moves machines professionally, Jim Steinhagen of Waconia, Minnesota, reviewed the section on moving equipment. Another local, Curtis Lundeen of Mayer, Minnesota, an avionics repairman, reviewed the section on electric motors.

Preface

The most beautiful printed text is produced with traditional letterpress, a process that gives the printer enhanced control as designs are developed, and guides the printer to legibility and a relaxed laying out of words.

In letterpress, proofs show faithfully the play of light on the page, rather than on a computer screen or on some type of intermediate proof; letterpress printers can use this to their advantage to obtain the exact, finished feel that they want. When the impression in the paper is strong and noticeable, the effect is rich and sculptural. I have long believed that the three-dimensional effect makes letterpress printing easier to read because the eye focuses on letters that lie below the surface of the paper, leaving the paper surface itself outside of the focal plane.

Preparing letterpress type is a slow, labor-intensive process; printing from type involves machinery and techniques on the fringes of today's world. Unlike type derived from computers and laser printers, hand-set type is expensive to acquire, and it takes up lots of room. The typical letterpress shop holds only a hundred fonts, while large institutional shops may have a thousand fonts. Further, the selection of type available from typecasters today is relatively limited. This apparent disadvantage has the benefit of compelling the designer to take a careful approach to spacing, color, ornament, and rule in order to vary and improve the appearance of his or her work. It also requires the printer to choose well when selecting faces for the shop.

Today's letterpress printer is like the fine arts painter, whose demise was predicted when photography was invented: instead of disappearing, the craft has enjoyed renewed enthusiasm in a fashionable niche.

Museums, art centers, and libraries promote fine printing and the book arts with new vigor; the public recognizes the carefully crafted book or broadside as something unique. Many colleges offer courses in letterpress printing as part of their curriculum in art or literature, and four book centers have become regional centers of activity: The Center for Book Arts in New York, founded in 1974; the Minnesota Center for Book Arts, founded in 1985; the Columbia College Chicago Center for Book and Paper Arts, founded in 1994; and the San Francisco Center for the Book, founded in 1996.

While some supplies have disappeared from the market place, others have re-emerged. A New York tannery, for example, is now marketing parchment for letterpress made from goat, calf, and deer skins. A network of private typefounders, centered around the American Typecasting Fellowship, continues to cast type, and a few typefounders are designing new faces. One heavy platen printing press (the Kluge) is still being made, but proof presses and table top platens are only available on the used market. Fortunately, these machines are very durable and will last for centuries. If interest in the art continues, it is likely that small presses will again be manufactured.

This manual is based on my experience teaching at the Minnesota Center for Book Arts in Minneapolis. I hope that those learning the craft will be able to supplement the information here with good advice and actual demonstration by an experienced printer.

The use of type is traditional, and my approach to typography is traditional. But the information on printing in this manual is written for those working in letterpress today. The manual applies the measurements used in the United States and refers to the supplies available here. Two glossaries in the back of the book will explain unfamiliar terms. One lists words related to paper, and one lists words related to printing.

LETTERPRESS PRINTING

1

Letterpress Printing

Letterpress printing uses three-dimensional type to transfer ink to paper, often with a rich, embossed result. It is practiced today by hobbyists who enjoy its tactile nature, and by artists and fine printers who prefer the embossed effect and the traditional appearance. It was once the most common method of printing.

Letterpress printing originated in Europe in about 1450, with antecedents in the Orient that are much older. Johann Gutenberg is credited with inventing *moveable* type in about 1450; he was the first to create a system of individual letters that could be assembled into text. Prior to Gutenberg, text for printing was carved into blocks of wood. According to historical theory, the invention of moveable type changed the dynamics of the Western world by making written communication widespread and unvarying from copy to copy.

When relief printing doesn't involve type, it is technically not a letterpress process. However, as other methods of converting text into relief surfaces, especially photopolymer, have become more common, the term *letterpress* has been applied to any relief surface used for printing text. Some use the term today as a substitute for *relief.*

Relief printing uses a raised surface to transfer ink to paper. Linoleum cuts, wood engravings, woodcuts, type, and photopolymer plates are all used in *relief* processes.

Relief printing is ancient. It is one of five important printing processes, including *intaglio, lithography, xerography,* and *serigraphy.*

Other kinds of printing

Intaglio printing, which dates from about the same time as letterpress, uses etched or engraved lines below the surface of a plate to transfer ink to paper. It is commonly called etching, engraving, or copperplate printing.

Lithographic printing uses the chemical separation of ink and water, usually on a metal plate, but sometimes (and originally) on stone. Because of the chemical separation, new ink rolled over the plate or stone adheres only to the original image, and the ink can be transferred to paper. Lithography was introduced in about 1800, gained prominence about 1850, and began to supplant letterpress in about 1960. Today, most of the world's printing is lithographic. If the ink is *offset* from the lithographic plate onto a rubber surface before being transferred to the paper, the process is called *offset printing.* As a commoner, it is fine to confuse *offset* and *lithography,* but as a printer, it is better to understand the difference.

Xerographic printing uses light to create an electrical charge on a surface; the electrical charge attracts toner, and the toner is transferred to paper and melted on to it. Laser printers and copy machines are xerographic; the term comes from the name of one of the first commercial copy machine makers, the Xerox Company.

Serigraphic printing uses screen-mounted stencils through which ink is transferred to paper. The process is often called *silkscreen.*

Printing press terms

Presses are typically classified as platen, cylinder, or hand presses. A platen press is a press with a flat platen that carries paper to type mounted on a bed; a cylinder press uses a rotating cylinder to carry paper over type mounted on a bed; a hand press carries paper on a frame over the bed between a horizontal platen and a horizontal bed. Hand presses are always powered by hand, but platens may be powered by foot, hand, and motor, and cylinder presses may be powered by hand or motor.

The term *letterpress* refers to a *process,* and shouldn't be applied to the *printing presses* used in letterpress printing. More correctly, these are called *letterpress printing presses.* Further, the term *printer* refers solely to a human being, never to a machine.

Regardless of the process, printing is called *hand printing* when the press or apparatus is powered by hand. A press is called *hand-fed* when paper sheets are individually fed to the press by hand, and *automatic* when the machine feeds itself. A *sheet-fed* press prints on individual sheets of paper; a *web* press prints on a stream of paper from a roll, which is usually cut into sheets as it is delivered from the press.

When a letterpress printing press has the type surface mounted on the curved surface of a cylinder, it is called a *rotary* machine. When a printing press prints on both sides of a sheet, it is called a *per-fecting* press.

The term *letterpress* is sometimes used by book-sellers and historians to describe a copy of a handwritten text, especially a letter. In the era of business handwriting, a *letterpress copy* was produced by pressing a damp sheet of paper against a handwritten original in a copy press. To make the text right-reading in the copy, thin paper was used, and the copy was read from the reverse side.

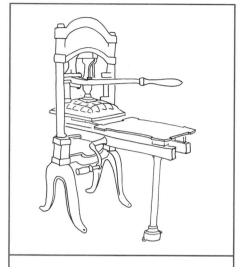

FIGURE 1
Hand press made by
Paul Shniedewend in Chicago

Why letterpress endures

We can categorize letterpress printers today as technologists, artists, cheapskates, or expansionists.

Technologists are intrigued by the technology, especially the handling of type, the working of the presses, or the inherent beauty of the equipment. Included in this category are many collectors who are fascinated with the design of metal and wood type.

Artists use the unique properties of letterpress to produce fine or artistic printing, including some who want to control the printing process for artistic or editorial reasons.

Cheapskates want an inexpensive means of reproduction. Because letterpress is more labor-intensive than offset lithography, it's become rare as a commercial process. As a result, acquiring equipment for a working letterpress shop is considerably cheaper than acquiring offset equipment. This motive has become less important now that computers and photocopiers are ubiquitous.

Expansionists already work with a relief process, such as woodcut, and want to expand their repertoire to include letterpress.

A letterpress printer's skill

The art of letterpress printing is one of assembly and arrangement. The printer assembles paper, type, ink, and binding materials for artistic effect. In some of these processes, the printer acts passively, that is, the printer makes choices, but doesn't manipulate the implements of any craft. Unless the printer cuts punches or engraves mats to cast type, for example, or makes paper, the skill lies in the selection of the type and paper produced by someone else. More directly under the printer's control is the adjustment of inking and impression, the combining of fonts, the design of the margins, and the spacing between lines, words, and sometimes, between letters. These manipulations involve hand work, but the real skill lies in the eye.

Fine printing

The line between excellent printing and fine printing is a difficult one to define; Stanley Morison said simply: "the fine printer begins where the careful printer has left off." But Morison wrote these words before the technology of printing underwent the radical change from letterpress to lithography in the late twentieth century. In Morison's time, every printer was working in letterpress; today, only the careful are.

Much letterpress work being done today—especially in book printing—is part of the fine printing movement, a conscious effort to express the spirit of a text and its illustrations using the best printing possible. The fine printer is really an artist, akin to the etcher or lithographer who makes prints.

The private press

The *private press* is an ancient term among book collectors. Originally, it was applied to publishers who produced books not offered for public sale. Today such publishers are rare, and the term is used to describe those that print the works of their owners, or print works cherished by them. The designer Eric Gill described the private press as one which "prints solely what it chooses, and not what its customers demand of it, which is the case with a 'public' press."

The *livre d'artiste, the book arts, and artists' books*

Livre d'artiste is a term that originated in France in the late nineteenth century to signify books illustrated by artists. The books were normally not works of art in themselves, but *trade* editions intended for discriminating buyers.

The *book arts* is a new field with a fragmented following and a lot of debate about what it comprises. The works produced are often called *artists' books*. There is no consensus on the meaning of these terms, although everyone seems to agree that an artist's book is intended to be a work of art. Some definitions refer to the use of an inexpensive means of production, the inclusion of unconventional media, or an anti-market sentiment on the part of the maker.

The scholar Johanna Drucker has called the artist's book the "quintessential 20th century art type." In her *Century of Artists' Books,* she suggests that a book can be called an artist's book only when it "interrogates the conceptual or material form of the book."

In my view, a book is a gathering of leaves bound together in a cover which opens to reveal its contents. When a work of art can be unlayered, when it can be more fully experienced by handling, it is book art. When handling it divulges nothing, it is sculpture which contains a visual reference to books.

Kafka wrote approvingly of books that "wound and stab us"; Ezra Pound said a book should be "a ball of light in one's hands." Certainly, no other form of art is so layered, or so cryptic, as a book.

Unfortunately, the public is usually exposed to printed art through exhibits at art centers and museums, where books are treated as untouchable objects. To see a book on exhibit means, as a matter of course, to see it within a glass enclosure; the likelihood is remote that the book's experience, its unlayering, will ever be accessible.

2

Measurement

Most measuring is done in *picas*, an ancient measure, unique to printing, which converts imperfectly to the inch. A pica is about ³⁄₁₆ of an inch, and is quite close to 4 mm. The pica derives its name from a historical type face called pica, which was made in that size.

The pica is equal to 12 *points*. Points are used to measure the size of type and the thickness of rules, leads and slugs.

Measure a piece of type in points *pointwise*. Measure the spaces used with type in *ems*. The em is based on the width of the letter 'M,' which is generally cast on a square body of type. The em is equivalent to the vertical size of the type in points, so an em of six point type is six points wide and forms a square, measuring six points on each side.

Likewise, an 'N' is normally half as wide as it is high, so an *en* in six point type is three points wide. Spacing used with type is based on the em and

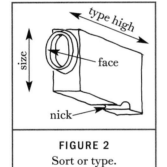

FIGURE 2
Sort or type.

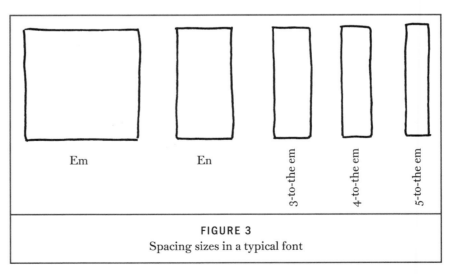

Em   En   3-to-the em   4-to-the em   5-to-the em

FIGURE 3
Spacing sizes in a typical font

en, and the typical font of type includes em, en, three-to-the-em, four-to-the-em, and five-to-the-em spaces. The em space itself is often called an *em quad,* and its multiples are called two-em quads, etc. The three-to-the-em, four-to-the-em, and five-to-the-em spaces are sometimes called simply "three-em *spaces*" etc. There are also *thin spaces* made of brass and copper; a brass space is twice the thickness of a copper space. Thin spaces are purchased separately from type.

The normal height of type (from the base to the printing surface) is called *type high,* and is .918 inches in the U.S., Canada, and England. In Europe, type height varies, but all European type is slightly higher than .918 inches. European type founders can usually adjust their machines to cast to (or mill to) the .918 standard.

Lines of type are now measured in picas. Type was once commonly measured in ems, with a line of six point type measured by the number of six point ems that were set, and compositors were often paid accordingly.

Measure a gathering of type (or *type block*) in picas, both horizontally and vertically, from the top to the bottom and from side to side. Measure *furniture* (or blocks of spacing material) in picas. Measure long spacing material such as *leads, slugs, and wood reglets* in picas for length, and points for thickness. A lead is a metal strip 2 points thick; a slug is a metal strip 6 points thick; a thin reglet is a wood strip 6 points thick, and a thick reglet is a wood strip 12 points thick.

Sometimes it's simpler to describe these thicknesses in picas, remembering that:

    a *lead* is 2 points, and three make half a pica

    a *slug* is 6 points or half a pica; *two slugs* are 12 points or one pica

    a *thin reglet* is 6 points or half a pica

    a *thick reglet* is 12 points or one pica

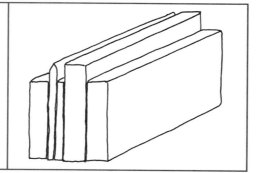

FIGURE 4
Spacing and rule. Relative sizes of common metal and wood spacing and rule. Left to right: a slug, a hairline rule, a lead, a 6 point rule, and a thin reglet. In thickness, these measure 6, 3, 3, 6, and 6 points, respectively.

(A one point lead is also made, but is not common.)

Combinations of leads and slugs can be used to form spaces in a line of type where a lot of space is called for, as shown in figure 15 on page 30. Since leads are two points thick and slugs are six points, they can be combined to form spacing for nearly all of the point sizes in which type is made.

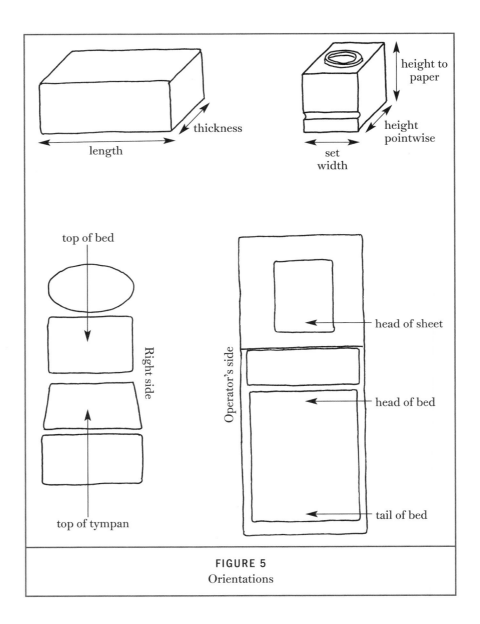

FIGURE 5
Orientations

The pointwise size of the type body on which the character is cast determines the nominal size of the type, that is, the size which that type is called. Though two fonts may contain *characters* of different sizes, both fonts are called 12 point if the *body of the type* is 12 point.

Occasionally, a face will be cast on a body for which it wasn't originally designed, in which case it is called *12 on 14* or *10 on 11*. Casting a face on a larger body is usually done as a means of leading, or increasing the line spacing, without having to insert leads.

It's easy to determine the size of type when the size is a multiple of 6 or 12, because its measure will correspond to the marks on a printer's ruler. Type that is 8, 10, 14, and 30 point will fall between the marks. You will quickly develop an eye for the various sizes of type.

The size of *wood type* is often measured in lines, with 6 lines to the inch. Occasionally one will see agates on a printer's ruler, an old standard which was still used to measure newspaper advertising a few decades ago; an agate is about ¹⁄₁₄ of an inch.

Letters: measuring their characteristics

Letters are positioned on an imaginary horizontal line that they appear to rest on, called a baseline. A number of measurements are made from the baseline, including: ascender height (the distance to the top of the ascenders); cap height (the distance to the top of the upper case letters); x height (the distance to the top of the lower case 'x'); and descender depth (the distance to the bottom of the descenders).

Rule

Rule is a type high strip which is used to print a line. The thickness of the face or printing surface is usually measured in points, as in *half point rule* or *one point rule*. When the thickness of the face exceeds a pica, it is measured in picas.

Paper

The dimensions of *paper* are measured in inches or centimeters, and its weight in *basis pounds* or grams per square meter. A full discussion of paper density or weight appears in the chapter on paper.

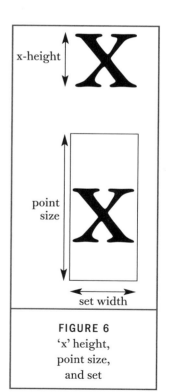

FIGURE 6
'x' height,
point size,
and set

Learning to measure by eye

One of the significant advantages of letterpress is the ease with which trial proofs are made on the actual stock selected for a project, using the same process that will be used for the printing of the edition. Such a proof is unusually faithful, and adjustments in the composition can be made with ease. Seeing the effects of all the components in their finished form, the printer can quickly and precisely react by adjusting margins, spacing, and overall tone on the press, before edition printing begins. Even the color of the ink can be adjusted in the proof stage.

The fidelity of the letterpress proof gives printers immense control over their product. To take advantage of this, the printer must learn to see prototype designs made by hand or computer as approximations, rather than as templates whose precise measurements are to be slavishly observed through the printing process. Letterpress printers should not anticipate the finished appearance of a composition before the project is even set into type, but should trust their eye to judge the final product, taking full advantage of the proofing process to perfect their work.

3

Type & Typographical Printing Surfaces

Type is a reverse-reading letter or character on a base that can be combined with other types to print words and sentences. It is made from either metal or wood. The word *type* signifies an individual piece of type, as well as a collection of types. An individual type is usually called a *sort*. Type is uniform in height from the base on which the type stands to the face of the character, so it can be arranged together to form a relief surface from which to print.

A *type face* is a series of letters of one particular design which has been cast or cut to form a printing surface. Type faces are often distinguished by the styling of their serifs, their shapes, and their weights (that is, the thickness of their strokes).

In letterpress, a *font* is an assortment of type of the same *face and size*; it is the *supply* of type of one kind for a particular shop. The concept is easy to grasp when one remembers that *font* also means spring or source, as in the phrase: *font of wisdom,* or the word: *fountain.* In recent years, of course, the term *font* has come into common use to signify what letterpress printers have traditionally called *face*.

Families of type are groups that include variations on a face. Garamond bold, for example, belongs to the Garamond family. Variations may include bold, condensed, italic, and outline.

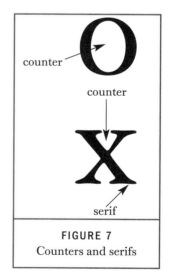

FIGURE 7
Counters and serifs

Classifications distinguish faces according to their overall characteristics. Classifications include roman, sans serif, decorative, gothic, and script. A serif is the line that terminates the linear strokes of the face. A *sans serif* face has no serifs.

In order to provide white space between letters, type is usually cast on a body that is slightly wider than necessary to contain each character. The width of the body of the capital 'M,' measured from left to right in points and fractions of a point, is referred to as *set*. When the set of a font is nominally equal to its point size, the face is normal. Occasionally, type is cast with the set increased by a small amount, to change the appearance of the type by spacing the letters apart. Such type is said to be *10 point 10½ set.* Monotype machines, discussed below, can be adjusted to vary the set.

Roman type faces are generally divided into old style and modern, signalling a change that occurred in about 1800.

OLD STYLE FACES HAVE

> *limited contrast between the thick and thin portions*
> *a noticeable slant in the axis of the thick and thin strokes*
> *bracketed serifs (that is, serifs with rounded braces joining*
> *   the stem and serif)*
> *capitals with distinct variation in width; 'B' is thinner than 'O'.*

MODERN FACES HAVE

> *distinct contrast between thick and thin parts of a letter*
> *an axis which is vertical*
> *serifs which are unbracketed hairlines*
> *capitals with less variation in width;   'B' is as wide as 'O'.*

A *counter* is an enclosed area of white within a letter form, such as the center of an 'O.' A counter was traditionally formed by driving a counter punch into the surface of the primary punch used to form the mat. After hardening, the primary punch, which carries the face of the letter in relief, is driven into a softer metal mat to form the surface against which the type is cast.

FIGURE 8
Old style and modern type designs:
upper case *O*s from Garamond (left) and Times New Roman (right).
The counter in the old style slants slightly, and there is less apparent contrast
between the thick and thin portions of the letter. The symmetry of the
new style designs gives them a more "machine-like" appearance.

Type makers commonly made subtle adjustments in the design of the face as the size varied, in order to adjust its overall appearance as the scale changed. Therefore, a face in 8 point which is enlarged optically will look different when compared with the face in 48 point.

Type has been made by many foundries, and type faces were called many different things; sometimes the *same face* was called *different names* by different foundries, and sometimes the *same name* was used by different foundries to describe *different faces*. Because of this, it is prudent to mention both the type foundry and the face when describing type.

Decades ago, the American Type Founders Company issued a series of "Printing Instruction Charts" that showed the lay of the case, how to hold the composing stick, etc. One of the charts, "Type Identification Aids," (figure 10) compares characters from several roman and sans serif faces side by side, showing the differences between faces with similar appearance. The placard suggests that each shop prepare a guide comparing its own faces. Such an aid would allow workers to identify type quickly and avoid mistakes when distributing. Unfortunately, I have never visited a shop that has prepared such a guide, including my own.

Working with type remains the best way to learn the nuances of letterpress, regardless of what methods one eventually adopts. The printer who has seen and dealt with the problems of uneven type, type off its feet, and work-ups, will be well equipped to solve problems when printing from polymer plates, for example.

The making of metal type

Until about 1630, printers typically cast their own type, making sorts one at a time in a small, hand-held mold. After 1630, the making of type became a specialty and printers generally ordered their type from foundries, though the typemaking process remained unchanged.

In the early 1800s, machines were invented to make type, and then machines were invented to compose the type into text. Finally, really workable machines were invented that arranged the casting mats in text order before the type was cast, so that type no longer had to be picked out of cases by hand; the arrangement of type into text occurred as the type was made.

Casting machines create type from molten metal, using a mold to form the sides, and a mat (or a matrix) with an engraved or punched character to form the face, or printing surface. Molten typemetal is pumped into the

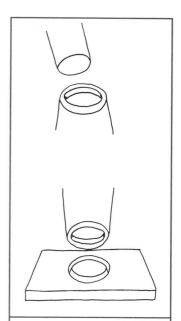

FIGURE 9
Punch and counter punch.
Above:
Forming the counter in a punch, using a counter punch. The punch, made of soft steel, is hardened after it is shaped.
Below:
Forming a mat with a hardened punch. Brass is typically used for a mat.

TYPE IDENTIFICATION AIDS

Certain characters in each type face have serif or body peculiarities by which the face may be identified. Study the comparisons below and make similar ones for faces in your shop.

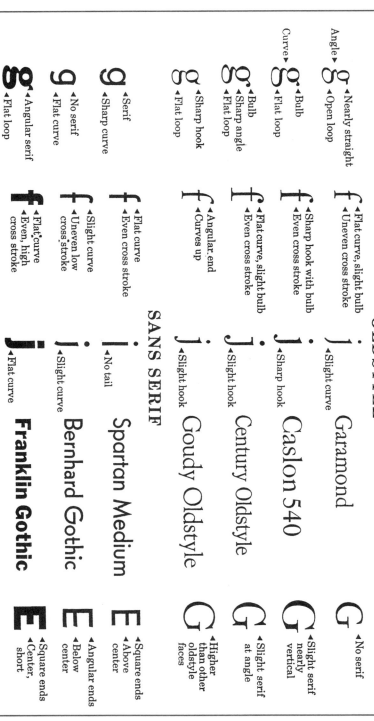

OLDSTYLE

g ◄Nearly straight	f ◄Flat curve, slight bulb ◄Uneven cross stroke	j ◄Slight curve	Garamond	G ◄No serif
Angle ► g ◄Open loop	f ◄Sharp hook with bulb ◄Even cross stroke	j ◄Sharp hook	Caslon 540	G ◄Slight serif nearly vertical
Curve ► g ◄Bulb ◄Flat loop	f ◄Flat curve, slight bulb ◄Even cross stroke	j ◄Slight hook	Century Oldstyle	G ◄Slight serif at angle
g ◄Bulb ◄Sharp angle ◄Flat loop	f ◄Angular end ◄Curves up	j ◄Slight hook	Goudy Oldstyle	G ◄Higher than other oldstyle faces
g ◄Sharp hook ◄Flat loop				

SANS SERIF

g ◄Serif ◄Sharp curve	f ◄Flat curve ◄Even cross stroke	i ◄No tail	Spartan Medium	E ◄Square ends ◄Above center
g ◄No serif ◄Flat curve	f ◄Slight curve ◄Uneven low cross stroke	j ◄Slight curve	Bernhard Gothic	E ◄Angular ends ◄Below center
g ◄Angular serif ◄Flat loop	f ◄Flat curve ◄Even, high cross stroke	j ◄Flat curve	Franklin Gothic	E ◄Square ends ◄Center, short

FIGURE 10

"Type Identification Aids": a placard issued by the American Type Founders Company.

mold with the mat at one end. After the type is cooled and solidified, a protrusion called a *jet* is broken off the bottom of the type, or the bottom is shaved clean with a blade.

For good results, type casters must operate at carefully controlled temperatures, pressures, and speeds. The variables in casting machine-made type include: the content of the typemetal and its temperature as the type is cast; the size and temperature of the mold; the pressure used to fill the mold; the position of the mat in relation to the mold; the position of the nozzle, which fills the mold with metal, in relation to the mold; the condition of the mat; and the adjustment of the trim knives which finish the type.

Type metal is mostly lead. Depending on the size of the type and the machinery making the type, the proportion of lead varies from about 50 to 85 percent; the proportion of tin from 12 to 44 percent; and the proportion of antimony from 2 to 28 percent. The antimony hardens the metal and makes it expand to fill the mold as it cools; the tin hardens the metal, bonds the different metals, and allows the mix to flow quickly. Lead is the main ingredient despite its relative softness; if the proportion of antimony exceeds about a third, the molten metal flows poorly.

Foundry type

Foundry type is the best of all type, with superior definition, hardness, and durability. Foundry type, cast one sort at a time, was first made by hand in about 1450. Since about 1850, foundry type has been produced on machines called pivotal casters, and later on a variety of improved machines such as the Barth caster.

DUENSING TITLING
ABCDEFGHIJKLMNOPQRSTU
VWXYZ& ÆŒ .,-:;'!?

FIGURE 11
New metal typefaces are occasionally introduced.
Jim Rimmer of New Westminster, British Columbia, recently designed and cast this face,
Duensing Titling, named in honor of his mentor, Paul Hayden Duensing.

The American Type Founders Company (ATF) was formed from twenty-three type foundries in 1892, and dominated the foundry type market in the U.S. for a hundred years. Its type can be identified by a face number cast on the lower case 'm' and the capital 'H.'

ATF failed in the 1990s, and the auction of its equipment, in August, 1993, is remembered as a chaotic affair, with a lot of irreplaceable material needlessly diverted to the scrap yard.

With the exception of a single foundry, the Dale Guild, no one is casting foundry type in the U.S. today. Foundry type must be set by hand, and is distributed back into cases when the printing is completed. Eventually, it wears out, and inconsistencies develop in weight and impression among neighboring sorts.

It can be difficult to tell the difference between Monotype and foundry type. Monotype tends to be more silver in color, and tends not to develop a blackish patina as foundry type sometimes does. Monotype generally has a single nick, but may have more; foundry type may have one or more nicks. A small pin, used to retain foundry type momentarily in the mold during the separation of the type and mold, leaves a small mark on the side of the type body. This pin mark is sometimes found on foundry type, but is seldom found on Monotype. With some foundry type, the pin mark incorporates marks, letters, or words that identify the maker.

Machine composition

The Linotype and Monotype are both casting machines that were invented in the late 1800s to set and cast type in text order. The Linotype assembles an entire line of mats and casts the line as a single casting. The Monotype casts one sort at a time.

Casting machines like the Linotype and Monotype speed up the assembly or composition of type, but they also provide new material that reproduces well, and they eliminate the need to distribute the type, or return it to the cases, for reuse. Instead, any unwanted, used material is melted down to form new type.

Both the machines and the type they produce are referred to as *Linotype* and *Monotype,* respectively.

The Linotype

The Linotype is a fast machine, and the casting of each line of type as a unified slug makes for very easy handling, eliminating much of the danger of the type toppling on the galley or working loose on the press.

Linotype is sometimes poorly *lined,* that is, the horizontal position of the letters is often inconsistent. But Linotype is usually newly cast and therefore consistent in impression and weight. Since the matter can be remelted easily for reuse, the cost of distribution is eliminated.

The Linotype, introduced in 1886, was principally used for book and newspaper work. The Intertype Corporation manufactured a similar machine beginning in 1912; type produced on Intertype machines is typically referred to as Linotype.

The Linotype company recommended one of the softest of the various typemetals: an alloy of 85 percent lead, 11 percent antimony, and 4 percent tin.

Most Linotype machines are operated solely from the attached keyboard; a few were made that could be driven by punched paper tape. A Linotype machine can, however, repeatedly cast the same line from an assembly of mats, if needed.

The Monotype composition caster

A Monotype *composition* caster produces pieces of type that, though individual, come from the machine as justified lines in text order that are collected on a galley. A galley of type from a Monotype composition caster is pretty much identical to a galley of type set by hand. Generally, the Monotype composition caster casts from 4 point to 12 point; but some faces are available to 24 point.

A composition caster is controlled by a punched paper tape that is created on a separate keyboard and then mounted on the casting machine. The paper tape directs a case of mats into the needed positions as the type is cast, so the type produced conforms to the keyboarded text. Monotype matrix cases, which are groupings of brass mats in a steel frame, typically hold three complete fonts, so that small caps, roman, and italic or bold types can all be produced in the same line. The keyboard operator, using a mechanical counting system on the keyboard, specifies the spacing needed to justify each line.

The Monotype control tape can be re-mounted on a caster whenever material must be recast. Because Monotype composition consists of individual sorts, corrections to the finished type can be made by hand. During the last decade or so, computers have been used to drive pneumatic plungers that take the place of the control tape, so that a caster can be operated directly from an electronic file.

Monotype sort casters

A Monotype *Display* caster (or Orphan Annie) makes type from 14 to 36 points, a Monotype *Thompson* caster makes type 14 to 48 points, and a Monotype *Giant* caster makes type from 14 to 72 points. Unlike the composition caster, the Display, Thompson and Giant casters make the same sort over and over again until the operator mounts a new mat on the machine. The type made by these machines is intended to be distributed into cases and set by hand.

Monotype is much like foundry type, though it is usually made of metal which is softer and wears more quickly than foundry metal. For general composition work, the Monotype company recommended an alloy of 72 percent lead, 19 percent antimony, and 9 percent tin. For stronger type that would be used for a large number of impressions, the percentages were 58 percent lead, 26 percent antimony, and 16 percent tin.

Monotype *composition* was designed to be used and then discarded, rather than distributed into cases after printing. In a *non-distribution* system, the time required to distribute type is saved, and the type used is always new. But Monotype in all sizes was also sold in fonts for hand-setting as a cheap alternative to foundry type.

Spaces from a Monotype composition caster can vary from the traditional sizes of em, en, three-to-the-em, etc. Although the caster *can* produce spacing in most of the traditional sizes, it normally produces spaces in increments of .005 of an inch. These non-traditional spaces can confound the typesetter who is handsetting from a Monotype font that was originally composed as text; he or she will encounter spaces that look like conventional spaces but which are, in fact, larger or smaller. If the font was cast as sorts, however, it should contain only spaces in the traditional sizes.

Ludlow

The Ludlow caster was widely used in the newspaper industry for casting headlines, and is still popular with bookbinders, rubber stamp makers, and foil printers. Though a simple machine, the Ludlow can cast type from 4 to

96 point. The mats are taken from cases and arranged in a stick before casting. Setting with the Ludlow system is faster than setting conventional type, and a few printers use the Ludlow to set straight matter.

Type as large as 216 point can be cast by placing the letters sideways on the slug. Faces larger than the 12-point mold are cast with the face overhanging the base on top and bottom. Blank slugs support the overhang. The Ludlow Typograph Company began making the Ludlow caster in 1912. Just before folding in 1986, Ludlow claimed that 16,000 of its casters were in use around the world. In 1920, the company purchased rights to the Elrod, a machine designed to cast leads, slugs and rules up to 36 point in 24-inch lengths.

Wood type

Wood is often used to make type larger than about 72 points in size. Metal can be cast up to 144 point, but special skill and equipment is needed. Darius Wells of New York is considered the first to mass-produce wood type in about 1827; he published the first known wood type catalog in 1828.

Wells worked with a router combined with a pantograph, a method of making wood type that has continued to the present time. In about 1880, according to company lore, Edward Hamilton was asked to make a few letters of large type for a poster, and he cut the characters out of hollywood on a foot-powered scroll saw, then glued the letters onto a block of wood. The letters printed well, and Hamilton began selling wood type to others. By 1900, the Hamilton Manufacturing Company dominated the wood type market in the United States. Today, the Hamilton Wood Type & Printing Museum in Two Rivers, Wisconsin, continues to make and sell wood type.

By convention, the side of the body of the uppercase 'A' is often marked with the maker's identifying stamp.

Scrap type

The printer should keep worn or unwanted type to trade with typecasters, rather than sending it to a scrapper. Scrap typemetal is now difficult to find; a typecaster will usually be grateful to receive typemetal in partial exchange for new type.

The various kinds of typemetal should be segregated if possible. Foundry type is best kept separate from Monotype, Linotype, and rule, slugs and leads. Try to remove brass and copper spacing before dumping type.

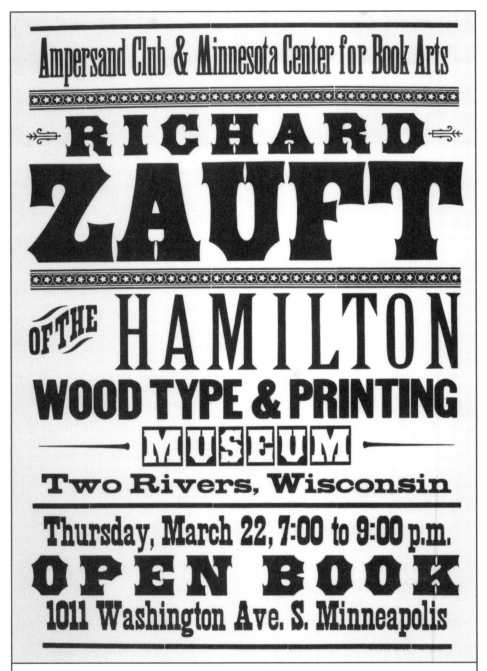

FIGURE 12

A 19 × 25 inch invitation printed from wood type in the author's shop, designed and printed by Paul Maravelas and Mary Jo Pauly in 2001.

A shop should have a *hell box*, a wood or metal container into which damaged type and various typemetal scraps are thrown. A practical final resting place for type is a five-gallon plastic bucket—the sort of thing used for bulk pickles and plaster. A plastic bucket filled with typemetal can only be lifted by two strong people; type in such buckets weighs about ten pounds per inch of height. Because the wire handles seem a bit light to be trusted with the weight of typemetal, I recommend lifting them with one hand on the bottom. The best container I have seen for typemetal is a wood box about 10″ × 10″ × 10″ with simple slats for handles; the box is easy for a single person to lift.

An impeccably clean wheelbarrow is a good receptacle when dumping type from a case, and if elevated on a ledge will dump its contents rather neatly into a bucket. A small rug or tarp can be used beneath the bucket to capture type that spills.

Stored metal should be kept clean and dry. Dirt is undesirable and can damage the typecaster. Water will encourage unwanted oxidation of the typemetal. A cover will prevent confusion about the purpose of the bucket; a bucket of scrap type buried under floor sweepings is a dismal sight.

Photopolymer plates

Photopolymer is a plastic that is changed from a water soluble state to a water resistant one with exposure to ultra-violet light. The change from water soluble to water resistant is commonly referred to as *hardening*. After the parts of a plate that are to print have been exposed, the unneeded portions of the plate are simply washed away with water.

Photopolymer could rightfully be called *photo-sensitive polymer*. Usually, the darkened portions of a photographic negative block the areas that are to be washed away, while the clear portions expose the rest of the surface to the waterproofing effects of light. The best results are had when the negative is held against the surface of the polymer plate in a vacuum frame while the plate is exposed.

After the unwanted portions are removed with water and the plate is dried, the plate is re-exposed to ultraviolet light to ensure that the polymer is as waterproof as possible. It is then mounted on a base to bring it to type height.

With a steel-backed photopolymer plate, a magnetic base can be used. If the plate is not backed with metal, it is mounted with adhesive, or with double-sided tape. Carpet tape and spray adhesives are commonly used. An unbacked plate is transparent, and allows the printer to see registration marks on the surface of the base when the plate is laid down. A problem with all mounting methods is that the plate may move during printing, especially if it is small and has a limited area of contact with the magnets or adhesive.

The Bunting base made by Bunting Magnetics in Newton, Kansas, is a popular base made of aluminum, with embedded magnets to hold metal-backed plates. Most frequently ordered are bases measuring 2 × 4, 6⅛ × 9 ⅛, and 8½ × 11¼ inches, and these sold in 2005 for $275, $588, and $818 respectively. Bunting will machine the base to any height, but most letterpress printers use a base .858 inches high, which they combine with a .060 inch plate to obtain the standard .918 inch printing height.

Another popular base is made by the Boxcar Press of Syracuse, New York, which uses adhesives to hold the plate. Their normal base is meant for a plate .037″ thick; the adhesive is said to add .004″ in thickness. Boxcar sells bases ranging from 4½ × 7½ with an etched grid on the surface for $150, to a 13 × 19 with grid for $575. Their bases without grids are about $60–80 cheaper than those with grids.

Some printers report satisfactory results in devising their own base. Typically, they obtain an aluminum base from a machine shop and glue magnetic sheeting to it.

On a platen press, a standard photopolymer base doesn't leave any room for gauge pins, so these must be placed away from the base where they will not be crushed. The plate can be mounted in the corner of the base nearest the gauge pins. If necessary, the paper stock can be cut larger than the finished size for printing, and cut down after printing.

Boxcar recommends that *deep relief* plates be used for platen presses, claiming that the form rollers may ink the relieved portions of a normal plate. Normal photopolymer plates have a relief of .027″, and a thickness of .037″. A deep relief plate has a relief of .045″, and a thickness of .060″; a thinner base must be used with a deep relief plate to make up the proper height to paper of .918″.

When mounting a plate, care must be taken that dirt and air bubbles aren't trapped beneath the plate. Plates are usually pressed down from one end to the other, to work out air as they're applied to the base. If bubbles of air are trapped, they can be forced to the side or brought through the surface by piercing the plate with a sharp tool.

Polymer plates are long-wearing, and cost about 50 cents per square inch. A few commercial shops will expose and wash plates for others. But the process is popular because much of it can be done by the printer, particularly if a vacuum frame is available to expose the plates. It takes some experience, however, to make good plates and to make them consistently.

The opacity needed for screening the plate surface from exposure is only available from a photographic negative. At present, a right reading negative with film emulsion up is usually used. The plates can be exposed briefly to normal light as they are handled before exposure. With films generated on a laser printer, for example, the black areas are imperfect, and allow spots of light to find their way through. *Direct to plate* exposure units are now marketed for commercial printers, which save the many steps needed in working with negatives to expose the plates. It is probably a matter of time before a method of screening and exposing a plate in a desktop laser printer is developed.

After printing, ink is cleaned from plates with typical print shop solvents, though alcohol should be avoided. Special solvents, said to be kinder to the plates, are also sold. There have been reports of allergic reactions to the acrylate in the polymer material.

Photoengraving

Photoengravings are made from plates of magnesium and other metals that are coated with a film of acid-resistant ground which is photographically sensitive; the parts of the ground exposed to light are insoluble. A photographic film is used to screen the ground; the unexposed ground is washed away, and the plate is bathed in acid. The acid etches away the exposed metal, but leaves the parts of the plate that are still covered with ground. The parts of the plate which are not etched are higher than the surrounding areas, and form the printing surface.

Magnesium is the most common material used for photoengraving today. The process is usually limited to shops that specialize in it for the printing trade. A magnesium photoengraving can carry a fairly fine line, and some printers prefer its qualities to those of photopolymer plates. Magnesium is also durable.

Commercial engraving shops can make engravings from flat art, negatives, and electronic files. These shops often mount magnesium photoengravings on a mediocre grade of plywood that varies in height from one corner to the other, and many problems in makeready result from this. Some printers obtain their photoengravings unmounted, and clamp them to a metal, honeycomb base, or use carpet-tape to mount them on a base of wood or metal. If photoengravings are to be mounted by the maker, it is helpful to have them mounted on blocks cut to pica widths.

After printing, the plates are cleaned with typical print shop solvents. A coating of petroleum jelly, applied before storing, will help prevent the metal from oxidizing.

4

Setting Type by Hand

Type is *set* or arranged into words and sentences in a composing stick from compartmentalized drawers called *cases*. A thin piece of typemetal, either a slug or a lead, is placed in the stick as the initial part of a support structure that will surround the type when it is moved. The setting begins with the first letter of the text, which is placed with the face of the letter out but upside down, and the side of the type against the left side of the stick. The next letter is placed to the right.

Three-to-the-em spaces are traditionally used between words, and *two* three-to-the-em spaces are placed after colons, semi-colons, question marks, exclamation marks and periods. Since about 1920, many printers have preferred to use four-to-the-em spaces between words.

By setting the type upside down and by beginning at the left, the type, which reads backwards, will be correctly arranged for printing. The typesetter begins by picking up a type from the case, rotating it until its nick is up, and placing it in the stick. To acquire speed, the typesetter should pick up each type and place it in the stick without looking at the face of the letter.

FIGURE 13
The composing stick in the hand.
The composing stick should be held this way, with the thumb holding the type against the side for stability. This method, which is awkward for beginners, should be practiced from the first; it will soon become comfortable.

When you have nearly filled the width of the stick with type, examine the line for mistakes. The nick or nicks on the type should match one another, and should be in line. Beginners will have to "mind their p's and q's," and it may be helpful to make a placard showing the orientation in the stick of the more confusing *demon characters:* d, b, p, q, n, u. A type which is from another font will likely have a nick or nicks in a different position on the type, and a sort which has been placed upside down in the stick will show a smooth side with no nick.

A good-quality tweezers is useful for picking up type in the stick and form. Be careful not to contact the face of the type with such a tool, as the type is easily scratched.

Large type is easier to work with than small; practice with 24-point type before you set six.

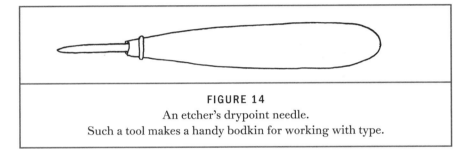

FIGURE 14
An etcher's drypoint needle.
Such a tool makes a handy bodkin for working with type.

Justification

Text is normally set centered, flush left (with a ragged right edge), or fully justified (with right and left margins flush). In all cases, each line of type must be spaced so that it is virtually the same length as the other lines in the type block.

The object is to make the line snug in the stick, and all of the lines equally tight. You should not be able to slide the type sideways and see more than a minuscule gap anywhere in the line, but the line should not be so tight that you must use a lot of pressure to force the last type or space into place.

As the type is set, three-to-the-em spaces are inserted between words. The occasional line will fit perfectly, with the end of the last word in the line neatly filling the stick. But most lines will require either an increase in the spacing between words, or a reduction in the word spacing already in the stick in order to make the line fit.

Some lines will require as little as a single copper thin space to make the line snug. Others will require as much as two three-to-the-em spaces between all of the words. More space than this usually looks excessive.

Part of the compositor's art is determining when to split a word between lines in order to fill a line so that spacing doesn't appear excessive. American convention is to divide most words according to pronunciation, while the British convention is to divide words according to their etymological components. Some dictionaries show how words should be divided.

Typographically, a minuscule word fragment should be avoided at the beginning of a line. Too many hyphens at the ends of lines become unsightly, and the occurrence of more than two in neighboring lines should be avoided.

Ampersands were once used to shorten lines that were too long by substituting the '&' for the word 'and.' But many readers today find ampersands awkward, and they are seldom used in straight matter.

Centered text

With centered text, the line is set with the first sort resting against the stick's knee. When the text is complete, the type is moved to the center of the stick, and spaces are added equally on both sides of the text until the line is snug. Place smaller spaces, which are liable to topple, on the inside, and larger, more stable spaces, on the outside of the line.

Flush left

With a flush left and ragged right margin, the line is set until the width of the stick is nearly full of type, and spaces are added at the end of the line to make it snug.

Since the position of the right edge is loosely defined in ragged right text, it is tempting to avoid dividing the final word of a line, especially when one isn't sure of where to correctly divide it. Excessive white space at the end of lines can result. To avoid this, the typesetter should determine a *minimum* line length before starting; if a line is short of this minimum line length, the next word should be divided.

Again, place any smaller spaces on the inside of the line, and larger spaces on the outside.

Fully justified

With text that has even margins right and left, you must determine where to cut off the text as the line nearly fills the width of the stick: you will normally be *short,* with too little type to fill out the line, or *long,* with too much type to fit.

When the line is short, you must decide whether to add text and reduce spacing, or add spacing to fill it.

To add text, decrease the space between the words you have set in order to fit the next word—or part of the next word—into the line. Often, the next word must be divided.

To add space, you normally add small spaces to those already in the line. Occasionally, you must remove the spaces already there in order to replace them with something larger. One method is to roughly gauge the amount of space needed to make the line snug, and divide that amount by the number of spaces between words. If a line is short by about an em, for example, and it has four breaks between words, then a four-to-the-em space can be added between each word.

FIGURE 15
Leads, slugs, and spaces from larger fonts can often be used for filling out lines.
Left, some three-to-the-em spaces from a font of 36-point type, turned on their sides,
fill out a line of 12 point type. Right, two slugs are used.

Adding a quad to the outside margins

To make their lines more stable for handling, some typesetters customarily place an em quad at the beginning and end of each line, a practice especially fruitful for very small type. If you adopt this practice, you will likely have to acquire a supply of extra quads.

Spacing

Again, limit space between words to about two three-to-the-em spaces; more space than this will appear excessive.

It's fine to vary the amount of space between words in the same line, but avoid different amounts of space on either side of a short word, where the variation will be obvious. Variations are less apparent when extra space is placed between adjoining words with tall terminal and initial ascenders. Extra space added between sentences, or after colons and semi-colons, is usually not noticeable.

Spacing contiguous upper case letters

Type is *letter spaced* by inserting space between individual letters. This is an important technique when whole words are set in upper case letters. If not done, the white space around individual letters will appear unbalanced.

The practice of balancing is best done by making a series of proofs and testing the visual results as the spacing is adjusted. When setting type

---

WAYZATA

With letters closely kerned together, this word is difficult to read. Modern signmakers often arrange words in this way. Letterpress type cannot fit this closely together without kerning, which requires special equipment.

WAYZATA

Set in unspaced type, this word shows a substantial amount of white space between the first few letters, while several of the letters in the center of the word appear crowded together. The word as set is not balanced visually.

WAYZATA

To correct this, a substantial amount of space was inserted between the letters 'YZ,' and a small amount was inserted between 'ZA.' The word appears more natural and relaxed.

WAYZATA

As an alternative to the deliberate letter spacing shown above, an equal amount of space has been added between all letter pairs. With this amount of letter spacing, the word still looks unnatural, but if more space were introduced, the word would appear balanced.

FIGURE 16
Letterspacing upper case letters

which you know will be adjusted after proofing, add some small spaces near the outside of the lines which can be moved between the letters as proofs are made.

One approach is to insert space between all the letters uniformly; when enough space appears between letters, small differences in white space cannot be seen.

Leading

Leads, inserted between each line of type, make the type easier to handle. The individual types slide across the stick more easily, and the additional white space is often welcome. Lines can be double-leaded and even triple-leaded. Generally, increased leading provides increased elegance and a more traditional appearance.

Before use, I try to put all leads and slugs *through the stick* in my shop, meaning that I set the stick to the line measure, say 20 picas, and place the leads and slugs in the stick in groups of about ten to make certain that none are longer than the lines of type. If any are too long, I will see the problem before I use them. Long leads or slugs do not allow the pressure of the quoins to be distributed to the type, resulting in loose lines in the form.

The composing stick

Composing sticks are either fixed or adjustable. With adjustable sticks, a lever normally frees the knee and allows it to be moved to a new position. When re-clamping the knee, make sure the teeth are correctly engaged in the notches of the stick.

Sticks for the left-handed do exist, but are so rare that in 1986 *Type & Press* published an article titled "Printer's Myth or Reality?: the Left-Handed Composing Stick." Unfortunately, left-handed printers must choose whether to devote their more dexterous hand to holding the stick efficiently or to setting type. In the latter case, the stick must be held awkwardly in the right hand. There is no reason why an industrious person couldn't commission or manufacture their own stick.

Adjustable composing sticks are often fitted with a tiny lever which will move the knee one half pica, adding an additional half pica to the line measure. H.B. Rouse, one of the largest manufacturers of sticks, numbered both the stick and the knee. To ensure perfect calibration, the two serial numbers should match.

If there are repeated problems with varying line lengths in your work, suspect either the consistency of your various sticks or their squareness. If the job has been set with more than one stick, there may be differences between the two that result in incompatible line lengths. Or a stick may not have parallel sides, so the last line that you set in the stick will seem as tight as the first line but will, in fact, be longer or shorter.

Check for inconstancy between sticks by comparing the tightness of the same line of spacing in both sticks. Check for parallel quality in a single stick by filling it with large quads, say 24 point, and observing the tightness of the lines as you complete them.

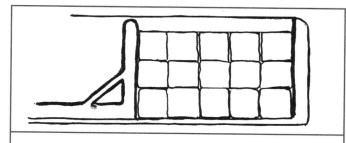

FIGURE 17
Checking a stick for squareness.
Check a composing stick for squareness by filling it with quads. Quads can also be used to set the knee of a stick that isn't graduated.

The type case

The most common case used in the U.S. is the California job case, which measures about 32 inches wide and is designed to hold a full font of type. A job case, which holds both lower and upper case letters, is sometimes called a *double case*.

A *two-thirds case* is about 22 inches wide and intended for small amounts of type.

A *split case* or *news case* is the same size as a California job case, but has one case for the upper case type and another for the lower case; a split case is used when a large amount of type will be set. The upper case contains capital letters, and the lower case contains lower case letters; they are positioned for typesetting on the cabinet as their name implies, with the upper case above the lower. Cabinets usually contain steel brackets or wood shelves on which the cases can be held. Because the compartments of a split case are larger than those in the other styles, a split case is a pleasure to use.

For the hand-setting of books, about 500 pounds of type—enough to fill several sets of split cases— is a prudent amount. The amount of type needed, of course, depends upon the number of pages that are printed at one time. Before the printing of a sheet begins, enough pages must be set for the printing of both sides of the sheet.

The three common types of cases (the two-thirds job, the California job, and the split) vary the position of the capital letters in relation to the lower case letters, but the arrangement of the letters within the two parts is constant. The lower case letters are arranged according to the frequency of use, with the most commonly used letters arranged around the center. The size of each compartment reflects the typical demand for a particular letter, because more types or sorts must be provided for the letters used most frequently. The lower case 'e,' for example, is the most frequently used sort, and is held in the largest compartment.

The form of our letters is much older than printing; our capital letters, or majuscule, date from Roman times, while our lower case, or minuscule, originated in about 800 A.D. The printer's upper case is arranged in alphabetical order from 'A' to 'Z,' with two letters, 'J' and 'U,' placed after 'Z.' The 'J' and 'U' were late additions to the Western alphabet, the 'J' first used in Spain before 1600, the 'U' in use in Italy by 1524; to express them, printers had previously called upon the 'I' and 'V.' The arrangement of the case has never been adjusted to accommodate the newcomers in their proper places.

The lay of the case should be memorized through use, with a diagram mounted in view while working. Some printers find mnemonic phrases helpful, such as "villains usually take three-ems and run," and "let me now help out your punctuation with commas."

Diagrams often show the *comma* and the *apostrophe* in this way:

comma   apostrophe

With most fonts, the comma and apostrophe are used to form quotation marks: a pair of commas is turned upside down to form the opening mark, and a pair of apostrophes forms the closing. Some fonts, however, are provided with specialized sorts for this.

Spaces are arranged in ascending order from left to right, with en spaces to the left of em spaces, and five-to-the-em spaces to the left of four-to-the-em spaces.

A few characters are seldom used, and are kept in obscure places, including the letter 'k.'

The ligatures 'fi, fl, ff, ffi' are much more beautiful than their corresponding forms 'fi, fl, ff, ffi' where the serifs, the dots, and ascenders are smashed together. In metal type, this "smashing together" is literal, and will cause part of the face to break. Ligatures should always be used with these combinations.

There are cases designed for foreign languages, music, figures, rules, and leads. Some cases were made to accommodate capitals, small capitals, and lower case sorts together. The American Type Founders' catalog of 1912 offered cases in nearly 60 different formats. But three formats are usually found: the California job, the two-thirds, and the split.

It often happens that a font contains more sorts than a case provides compartments. For this situation, use card stock to divide the compartments, and mark the unusual character on the card.

Cases for wood type

Wood type is usually kept in undivided cases called *blank cases*, and arranged in simple alphabetical order. The type is stored on its feet, with the face visible.

Cabinets for type cases

Case stands are simple frames without solid sides or backs in which cases are shelved with a bit of space between them. They usually date from the nineteenth century. Because the cases are open to the air on all sides, a lot of dirt gathers in them, but case stands seem to discourage mice from nesting.

Closed cabinets, with solid sides and backs, are made in both wood and metal. Metal cabinets seem to discourage mice from nesting. Because the cases in metal cabinets usually have a metal surface on the bottom which slides against a metal rest, heavy cases slide in and out of the cabinet more easily.

Keeping type cases clean

Type cases should occasionally be blown free of dirt and dust with a bellows or air hose. It is unhealthy to inhale typemetal dust, and such work should always be done out of doors.

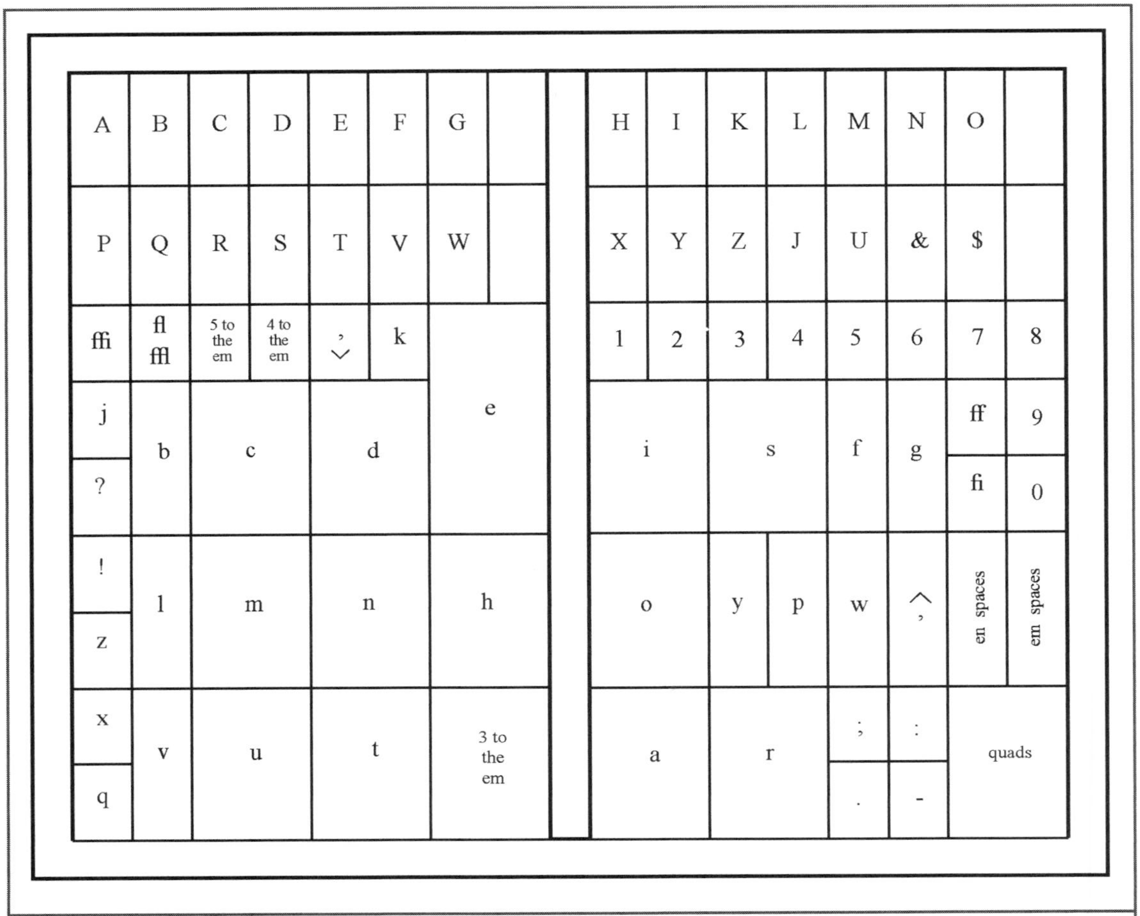

FIGURE 18

Lay of the case for the two-thirds case. The *California* style has eight compartments
in each of the four rows devoted to capital letters, as shown here. The *Yankee* style has seven.
The unassigned compartments in the California two-thirds case can be used for any sorts
that are needed but are not in the scheme.

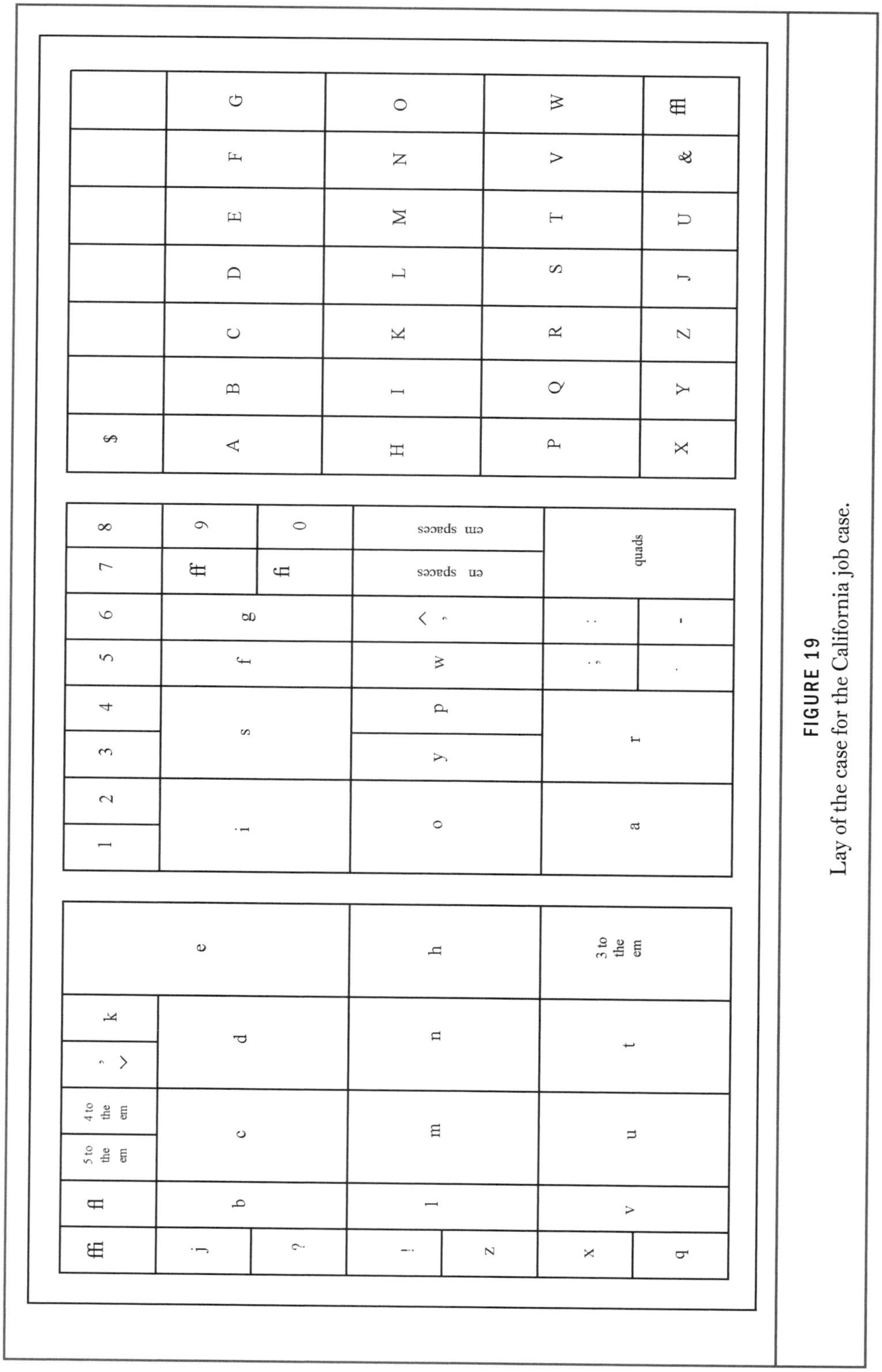

FIGURE 19

Lay of the case for the California job case.

*			G	O	W	)
1/4	1/2	3/4	F	N	V	]
1/3	2/3	&	E	M	T	U
1/8	3/8	5/8	D	L	S	J
7/8			C	K	R	Z
			B	I	Q	Y
			A	H	P	X

o			G	O	W	ffl
/			F	N	V	&
			E	M	T	U
%			D	L	S	J
@			C	K	R	Z
	—		B	I	Q	Y
	$	–	A	H	P	X

FIGURE 20

Lay of the case for the upper case of a split case. A series of small caps is kept on the left side. The case comprises a few lower case and miscellaneous characters, including the ampersand, one ligature (ffl), and two dashes. The empty compartments at the top are assigned to characters and symbols no longer in use, such as the ligature 'Æ'.

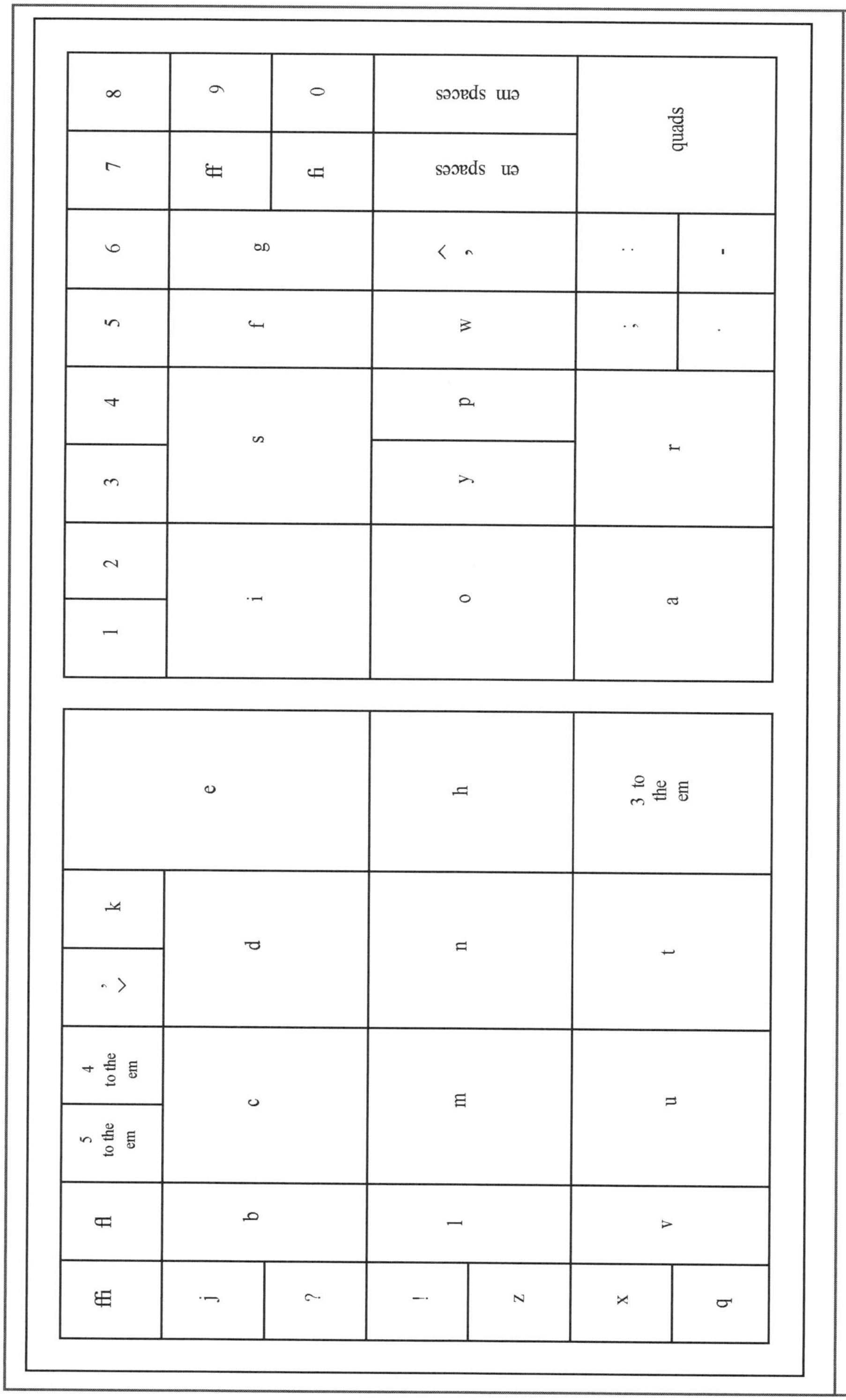

8 | 7 | 6 | 5 | 4 | 3 | 2 | 1

9 | ff | g | f | s | i

0 | fi | | | | o

em spaces | em spaces | ‹ › | w | p | y | a

quads | | ·· | ; | | r

| | · | ·

e | h | 3 to the em

k | d | n | t

· › | | |

4 to the em | c | m | u

5 to the em | | |

fl | b | l | v

ffi | j | ? | ! | z | x | q

FIGURE 21

Lay of the case for the lower case of a split case.

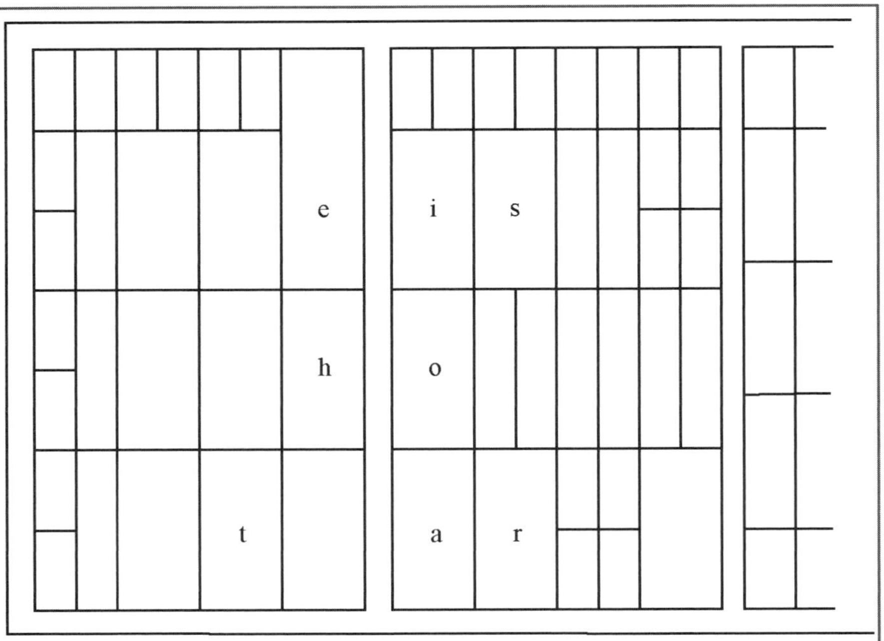

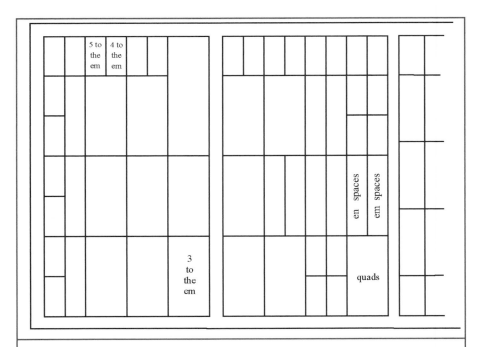

FIGURE 22
Lay of the case: Frequently-Used Letters
The most frequently used letters are grouped around the
center of the lower case arrangement.

FIGURE 23
Lay of the case: Spaces
Where spaces are side by side, they are arranged with the
smaller of the two spaces to the left.

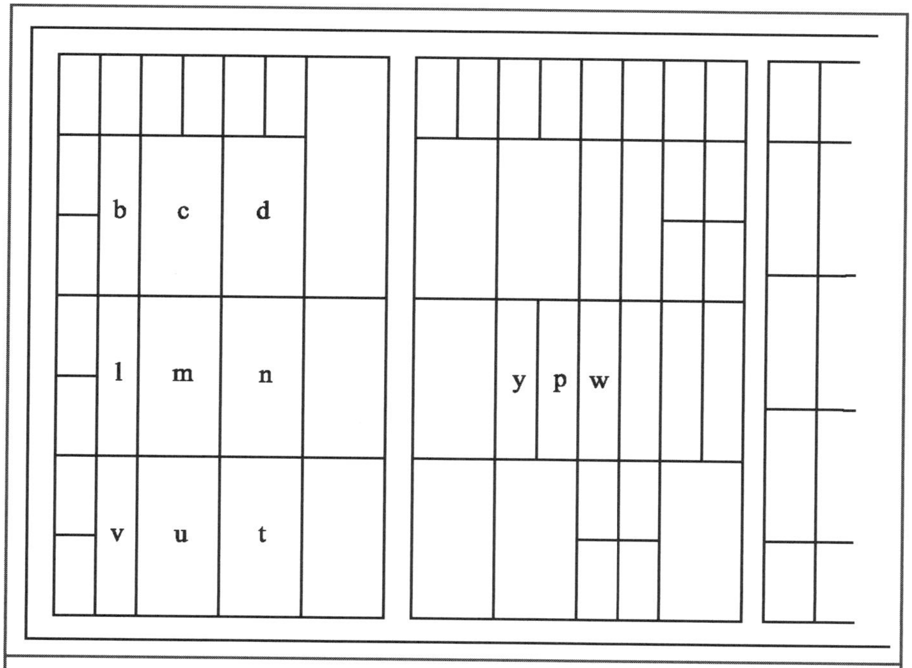

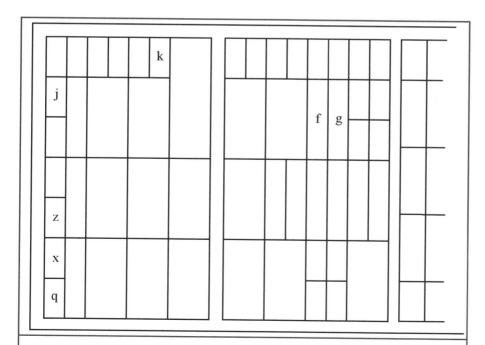

FIGURE 24
Lay of the case: Four Patterns to Memorize
Four patterns, when memorized,
help to locate many other letters.

FIGURE 25
Lay of the case: Obscure Characters
A handful of obscure characters
need to be simply memorized.

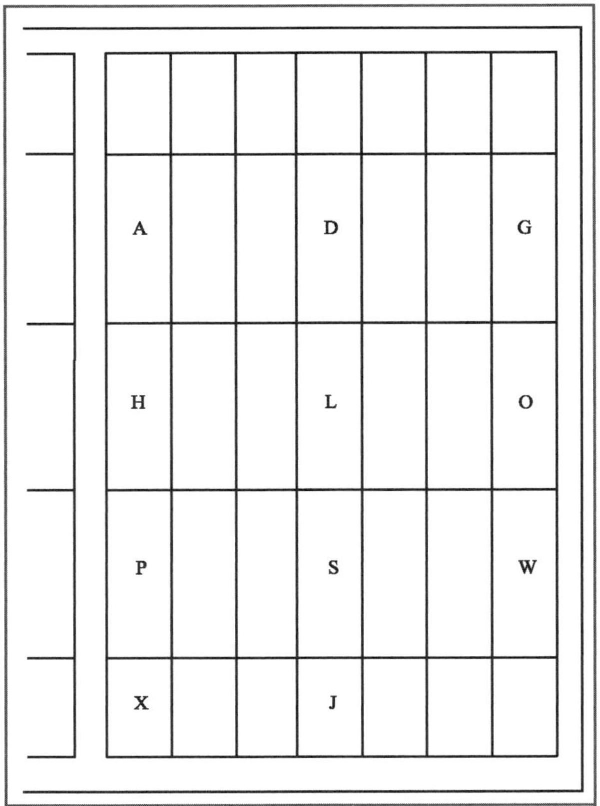

FIGURE 26
Lay of the case: Upper Case Guideposts
Knowing the first, middle, and last letters
in each row is a good way to orient oneself
in this part of the case.

5

Proofing Type

Type is proofed before printing to ensure that it is correctly set, to see and correct the layout, and to reveal any defects in the type, such as letters from another font, or worn or broken letters. A felt-covered planer, or a thin stack of paper beneath a conventional planer, can be used to obtain a rudimentary proof from inked type that is simply tied up or propped up as a block, but a really faithful proof can only be obtained from a press, and most proofing today is done in this way. Some shops will have proof presses available for this, while others will use a single press for both proofing and production. To avoid inking and cleaning an entire press for a proof or two, one can hand-ink a form and obtain a satisfactory proof.

A hand cylinder press is very easy to use for proofing—this is, after all, what it was designed to do. A platen press is less suitable, because it requires a thorough lock-up to secure the type, and more work to mount and dismount the form. Before a workable proof can be made, a platen press may also require adjustments to the impression.

I worked for a while in a shop with only a platen press, but soon acquired a proof press and evolved a design method that depends on a series of proofs. I now literally build most of my designs beside the proof press, adding elements where I see too much white space, and adding space where I see overcrowding. The dimensions of the final sheet size are usually determined while I am proofing as well.

As I begin making proofs, I pencil needed corrections on the proof, circling any damaged letters or misspellings, and drawing small wedge-like ticks where letter spacing is needed. If I feel that rule or some other visual ornamentation is needed, I pencil something in to see how it affects the design. If I want to see how an ornament might improve things, I ink an ornament by pressing it against an ink roller a few times, and I stamp it onto the proof after laying the proof on a stack of paper for padding. The ornaments do not give a perfect impression in this way, but I can, in a moment, clearly see how the visual tone of the design is affected.

I retain all of my proofs until I begin production printing, so that I can compare proofs and change things back when my design takes a wrong turn. As in all creative work, I find it helpful to create a design in intervals, putting the work aside for several days in order to see it with fresh eyes. More comments on design are contained in the chapter titled "Planning the project," which begins on page 137.

6

Stonework & Lock-up

Stonework is the process of preparing a block of type for printing by arranging it, surrounding it with furniture to create a form, and locking it up. *Lock-up* is the process of preparing a form for mounting on a press, usually by applying pressure with quoins (pronounced like *coins*) until the block and furniture are rigidly held. Stonework is so-called because stone was commonly used as a working surface. Today, the surfaces used to prepare type are still called stones, though many are now made of steel. Type is *planed* or knocked down level before it is locked up.

Moving type from stick to galley

After you have nearly filled the composing stick, move the type to a galley, either by picking it up out of the stick, or by sliding it from the stick to the galley. If you lay the stick next to the galley, with the top edge of the stick against the edge of the galley, you should be able to slide the type easily from one to the other. Place the type in the galley with the first line at the top end, so that the subsequent lines will fall into their proper place. One side of the block of type should rest against the galley's side, and the other can rest against a heavy piece of furniture. A piece of furniture on the tail of the block will prevent the last lines from toppling.

It takes a little practice to pick up a block of type successfully. Be sure to exert even force on all four of the block's sides; too much force is counter-productive. Practice by lifting a block to a small height several times. You will know at once if the block is poorly constructed, with lines that are too loose or too tight, or with reglets, leads or slugs that are too long for the lines. At times, when line lengths are variable and the block of type can't be stabilized, you must place the type into the stick again and re-space the lines so their lengths are consistent. Do the same with the leads and slugs in and near the form, putting them through the stick to verify their length.

Quoins and furniture

For printing, the block of type is surrounded with furniture to hold it in place, and tension is applied in two directions from quoins which are expanded to lock everything in place. It is usually not necessary to surround large blocks, such as photoengravings or linoleum blocks that are printed alone; these can be held in place with furniture and quoins bearing in one direction only.

The three common types of quoins are wedge, speed, and Wickersham. Though wedge quoins are locked into their final positions with a key, they can be worked without a key during the proofing stage, when little force is needed; simple finger pressure is sufficient. They can speed up the work on cylinder presses during the proofing stage, when there are repeated changes in the form and the printer is making single proofs. Their disadvantage is that they tend to twist or turn the furniture as they are tightened. I usually use them for proofing a form, when I make them only hand tight, and then replace them with Wickershams when the form is ready for production.

Speed and Wickersham quoins open with linear, rather than sliding pressure. They both require a key. Speed quoins come in many different lengths. A Wickersham quoin, when the key is rotated beyond the full open position, will snap shut, painfully pinching the finger which strays into the gap. Speed and Wickersham quoins should be oiled occasionally.

Two small quoins or a single speed quoin are usually placed on the long edge of the block of type, and one on the short edge. If the block of type is large, more than eight inches or so, more quoins can be used. A hefty piece of furniture should be positioned between the block of type and the quoins, to ensure uniform pressure against the side of the block.

A key left standing in a quoin is very easily knocked down onto the type. This is fine for the key, which is made of steel, but disastrous for the type, which is made of considerably softer metal. It is a wise habit, when opening the form, to keep the key continuously in one's grip until it is removed

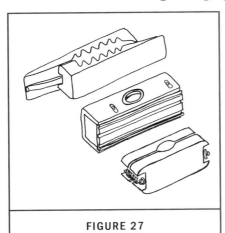

FIGURE 27
Quoins (top to bottom):
wedge, speed, and Wickersham.

from the last quoin and laid down on the furniture or bed until needed again, even if the form is opened for only a moment.

Furniture is usually made of wood, though furniture has been made of steel, aluminum, zinc, typemetal and plastic. Furniture can be homemade if necessary, but it should always be made in pica lengths.

Wood reglets and furniture can become warped or out of square. For this reason, use metal material directly around the block of type if possible, and suspect the wood furniture when struggling with a block of type that doesn't lock up correctly in the chase or on the press.

Furniture that is four picas wide is nearly square, and a groove is milled down the length of one side to indicate the top edge. This prevents the piece from being placed into the form on its side, which is only of consequence when the space needs to match another, either within the form or in some other form that must register with it. Nonetheless, it's wise to habitually place all four pica furniture into forms so that the groove can be seen on the top.

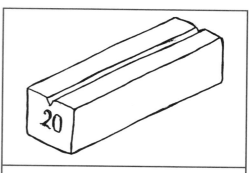

FIGURE 28
Four pica furniture.
Furniture which is four picas wide features a groove on one edge; place this in the form so that the groove is visible.

Platen presses

For a platen press, the type is moved from the stick or galley to an imposing surface. Some of these surfaces, called *stones,* have an indentation around them that can be used to hold a galley, making the galley surface level with the stone. When the block of type is on the stone, place a little furniture around it to keep the type from toppling, and unwind the string if the type has been tied up. The chase is then placed on the stone, surrounding the type block. On a platen press, the block of type is customarily placed on the press upside down, with the head of the block toward the bottom of the chase, so that the printed sheets are taken off the press right-side up, ready to read. Position the block of type near the center of the chase, with at least two inches of space between the block and the bottom of the chase so there is room for the gauge pins, which position the paper to be printed on the press.

The chase is filled with furniture and quoins, with quoins placed on the top and the right side of the chase. When the quoins are so placed, the top and left side of the block of type are consistently tightened against furniture whose position is fixed, no matter how many times the chase is lifted from the press and the quoins are loosened and retightened. The bottom and left

side of the form correspond to the sides on which the gauge pins are customarily placed; the relationship between the block of type and the gauge
pins should remain fixed by making those sides of the block rest against furniture, rather than quoins, since the quoins will vary in size according to the
tension to which they are set.

FIGURE 29
Lock-up for a platen press.
Filling the chase with long furniture, as shown, is the most dependable way to lock up. Platen press forms
are usually placed in the press with the type block upside down, and the quoins should be placed on the sides
of the block opposite those on which the gauge pins will be placed. If this form, for example, is mounted on
the press as shown, the gauge pins would be positioned on the bottom and left sides of the tympan. Since
wedge quoins tend to slide the type block sideways as they are tightened, the form will be less stable if the
block is pushed toward the other pair of quoins, where there is more spring. Orient wedge quoins so that the
quoin nearest the type block points away from the other pair of quoins.

Careful lock-up is required for platen press work, since the type is held vertically on the press. The type should be tested for integrity by lifting one side of the chase carefully off of the stone about half an inch, while pressure from the fingers is applied to the face of the type and the surrounding furniture. No type or furniture should be moveable during this test. If loose material is discovered, the quoins must be further tightened.

Hand cylinder presses

On a cylinder press, the type is usually placed directly on the bed of the press without a chase. The bed may have a lowered indention at the tail, so that the surface of a galley placed on it is level with the bed, and type can be easily slid between the two. The block of type is usually placed on the bed with the top of the block toward the *head,* or the end near the cylinder. Place a little furniture around the block to keep type from toppling, and unwind the string if the type has been tied up. Place some leads, slugs and reglets at the head and tail of your block of type to provide easy movement of the block longitudinally on the press. The extra spacing material can also be used to adjust the position of the block and the line spacing, to add rules or ornaments, or to change parts of the composition without disruptive changes in the surrounding furniture. For more details on positioning, see figure 42 and page 68.

Eyeball the position of the block on the press, which will determine, in part, the position of the block on the paper. First, position the feed board guide (the block on the feed table against which you lay the sheet), in a neutral position, so that it can be adjusted either right or left, and place a sheet of paper on the feedboard against the guide. If the sheet is small, correct the guide's position so that the sheet will be fed into as many grippers as possible on the cylinder. From the tail end of the bed, eye the position of the block, and center the block in relation to the paper. An assistant can help by adjusting the position of the block.

The block is then surrounded with furniture, with the quoins placed on the sides away from the grippers and side guide. The quoins are placed so that the sides of the block nearest the grippers and side guide are consistently pushed by the quoins against furniture whose position is

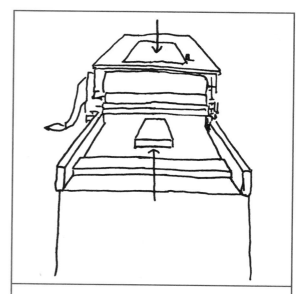

FIGURE 30
Setting up type block and paper. Position type and paper on the cylinder press by eye.

FIGURE 31

Lock-up for a cylinder press

The lock-up for a cylinder press should involve the longest furniture possible for stability. Note that the quoins are positioned to push the type block to the top and right; these sides correspond to the sides of the sheet positioned by the grippers and side guide. Extra leads have been placed above and below the type block to simplify adjustments in its longitudinal position.

If wedge quoins are used, orient them as shown so that any sidewise force is toward the rigid side of the form, which is filled with furniture.

fixed, even if the quoins are loosened and retightened. By making those sides of the block rest against furniture, rather than quoins (which may vary in size according to the tension to which they are set), the relationship of the block and the paper remains constant.

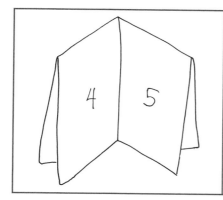

FIGURE 32
Mock-up for imposition.
Numbering the pages of a folded mock-up will show how type should be arranged or imposed on the bed. Remember that the pattern created will need to be reversed—think about how the type would see the sheet if it had eyes.

A removable *lock-up bar* is provided by the press maker to form the fourth side to the bed at the tail. With some presses, the bar ties into holes in the bed or the sides; with others, the bar expands to clamp to the sides. Some lock-up bars also produce pressure against the form, so no quoin is needed on the tail end of the bed.

Plane the block before printing.

Planing the type

With the type standing on a clean, level, and rigid surface, the quoins should be tightened so that they bear very lightly on the block of type—just tight enough to prevent the hand from sliding them sideways, but no tighter. The type is *planed,* or tapped down with a planer and a few very light blows to settle the type on its feet.

A planer of appropriate size should be used, that is, a small planer for a small block. Wipe the working surface clean of any grit before use. The planer should be set on the block and gently rocked to seat it; this will show if the planer is poorly centered on the block as well. A planer which is tapped without being seated squarely on the face of the type may batter it.

The planer is best held down on the type in one hand, squeezed between the thumb and forefinger, while a light mallet or even a quoin key is used to strike it.

After a light blow or two, the planer should be picked straight up off of the block; it should never be dragged across the face of the block, which

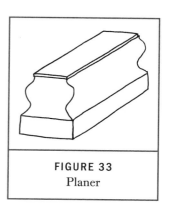

FIGURE 33
Planer

will do damage. A planer should be treated with care. Most printers set them down only on one of their sides, rather than their bottom, to avoid accumulating dirt and grit on the working surface.

After planing, a form is locked up by tightening the quoins until the form is firmly held. Normally, one side of the type block will compress considerably more than the other when the quoins are being tightened; tighten the quoin or quoins on that side first. The tightening of each quoin should be done in increments, as you tighten each in turn.

Excessive pressure from the quoins will lift the block of type from the stone or press bed as the quoins are tightened. It is also possible to break a chase with too much pressure. The quoins should be made only as tight as needed for locking-up.

Workups

Workups are individual types, spacing, or areas of a form that aren't locked up securely and that rise up from their neighbors during printing. Type which works up often brings with it spacing material which is eventually inked and printed. One of the dangers of workups is that the type or spacing can rise enough to be sheared off by the ink rollers or impression cylinder, then fall onto the block of type and damage it. Most workups result

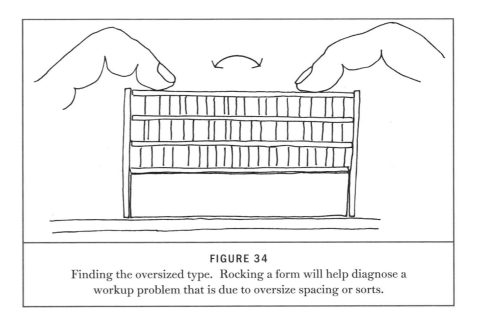

FIGURE 34
Finding the oversized type. Rocking a form will help diagnose a
workup problem that is due to oversize spacing or sorts.

from warped furniture, faulty spacing, or poorly justified lines. Soft under-packing beneath the type seems to contribute to workups.

Correcting these defects will usually correct the workup. Turning all of the furniture over will sometimes eliminate the problem. If all else fails, try inserting one of the following traditional cures into the type. *Sinkers* are made from two thin strips of cardboard with a thin thread mounted between them; the thread is positioned near the top edge and the two pieces of board are pasted together. Fine sandpaper and strips of cardboard have been used to even out pressures, as well as sharpened wood pegs made from matches or toothpicks, called *Dutchmen*. A more modern remedy is double-sided tape placed on the edge of a line of type.

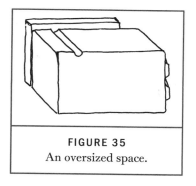

FIGURE 35
An oversized space.

An errant type can cause looseness in the form

Sometimes it is impossible to make an individual line tight with the quoins. One cause is a space or a type that is larger pointwise than the material around it, and which bears more than its share of the pressure from the quoins. The resulting curve in neighboring rule or leads can sometimes be seen, especially when sighting down the length from the side. A pointed tool can be used to detect such a space or type when the type is locked up and lifted from the stone, since the offender will be rigidly held in place while the type around it is loose.

Mitered borders

It requires a little experience to arrange a four-sided border with mitered corners around a block of type. Each side of the border must be long enough to close at the corners as the quoins squeeze everything together, or the resulting gap will be unsightly. If the border is cut too long, the border material will bear more than its share of the pressure and the block inside the border will not be properly compressed.

A miter trimmer is used to shave the corners to a 45 degree angle. The trimmer should be placed near the form when fitting borders, and the form should be locked up in a chase that can be lifted to check for integrity. The type within the border will compress in both directions, though mainly along the longest axis, and any gross deflection of the border can be seen by sighting down the border when the quoins are tightened.

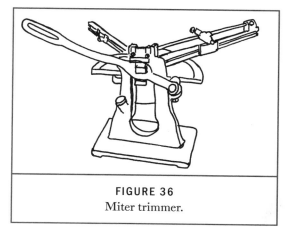

FIGURE 36
Miter trimmer.

Storing type

Type that is left standing for future printing or distribution is traditionally stored on steel galleys, although older, wood galleys are sometimes found. Galley cabinets hold fifty or more steel galleys. Use care when pulling galleys out from the cabinet to inspect them, as it is easy to let the end you are holding drop down, and the other end rise up and strike the galley above, smashing the type. To protect the type, some printers place a piece of wood that is higher than the type across the back of each galley. Unlike most printers, I shelve my galleys with the lip deep inside the cabinet, where it prevents the type from falling off as the galley is moved in and out.

Galley magnets will secure a block of type nicely on the galley; the ones specially made for printing are strongest. Galley springs are strips of spring steel that are wedged against the sides of the galley; they are less secure than magnets.

Type stored on galleys for long periods of time can be tied up with string. To tie type, use a strong, thin string, and make tight, orderly wraps around the block from the bottom to the top. A traditional method of securing the string at the beginning and end of the wrapping makes for easy unwrapping: at the beginning, secure the end of the string by overlapping it several times. After a few wraps are started, apply a lot of tension to the string as you make the wraps. When twenty or so wraps have been made, turn the last corner and shove the end down between the wraps and the block with a lead or other thin object, leaving the very end exposed as a grip for the future, when you want to pull the wraps apart.

Do not leave type stored in a platen press chase for more than a week. The furniture, especially when made of wood, will inevitably contract, and gravity will pull the type apart.

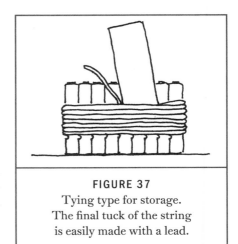

FIGURE 37
Tying type for storage.
The final tuck of the string
is easily made with a lead.

Transferring type from case to case

A transfer case is used to move type from one case to another by inverting the cases as they are held together. One is easily made.

Remove the bottom from a matching case, and sand the sides and dividers from the top—the previously open side—down to the level of the small partitions. Cover the *top* with plywood or heavy window screen. Screen helps to rid the type of dust and dirt during transfer. Nail battens over the screen to hold it in place, and nail the screen onto the partitions with small nails. Hot glue may also be used. With screws, attach a wood frame that extends to cradle the mating case around the four sides.

In use, the transfer case is placed over the case containing the type to be transferred, and clamped in placed with wood-working clamps. The two are then inverted, and the type falls from the original case into the transfer case. The process is repeated to move the type from the transfer case to the new case.

Fonting type

When all of the type is taken out of a case and tied up as a block, it is *fonted*. The type is usually put in alphabetical order using a composing stick. It is a time-consuming process, especially for small type.

Travelling with type

A block of type can be tied securely with string and placed in a square tin. The block should be surrounded with furniture and covered with rags.

7

Cleaning & Distributing Type

General safety

Concerns are growing about the health effects of common solvents, and printers should take some simple precautions when working with them. A discussion of solvents follows, in the chapter titled "Safety."

Cleaning metal type and plates

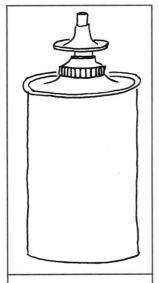

On a cylinder press, type and plates are normally cleaned while still on the press. On a platen press, the chase is removed to a stone. In both cases, the type or plates are left locked up.

Solvent is normally poured on a rag rather than directly on the type or plate, since little solvent is needed to remove ink from these surfaces.

Solvents designed for cleaning metal type are commercially available, but most printers are content with mineral spirits, which is effective and relatively safe, in terms of fire, toxicity, and reactivity to vinyl, urethane, composition, and rubber rollers. Odorless mineral spirits is also available.

When quick drying is required, such as when cleaning a form in the middle of a press run, use varnish maker's and painter's naphtha, often marketed as *VM&P naphtha*. VM&P naphtha is more flammable than mineral spirits.

When ink dries on presses, type, or tools, lacquer thinner will remove it. Lacquer thinner is a mixture of toluene, acetone, ethyl acetate, alcohol, and other distillates, and it is toxic and flammable.

Lye, gasoline, and kerosene were common solvents in the shops of former times. All of these had disadvantages. Lye is caustic and dangerous to handle. Gasoline is extremely flammable. Kerosene is toxic, and requires a lot of time to dry.

FIGURE 38
Brass solvent can.

Cleaning wood type

Special solvents used to be sold for use with wood type, but they are now difficult to find. The American Wood Type company used to recommend *benzine* (or white gas) as a solvent. If none of these are available to you, a very small amount of mineral spirits on a rag should be used. The type can also be cleaned with a soft, dry rag.

Numbering machines

Numbering machines require a specialized solvent that both cleans and lubricates the machine.

Distributing type

The printer first makes certain that the type to be distributed belongs in a particular case by holding a few sample sorts from the case and from the form side by side, and comparing the size, the nicks, and the faces.

A small quantity of type is taken into one hand with the face of the letters visible. The hand is moved around the case and the sorts are dropped one at a time into the compartments, without regard to orientation. Care is taken not to drop the type onto its face, which is easily dented.

Some very large faces are arranged on their feet, since more type will fit into the case that way.

Some printers like to distribute used type into a different case, in order to rotate it in terms of wear and to prevent some type in the font from being used repeatedly while other type is never used. This practice is used mostly with new type.

8

Press Operation

Generalities common to platen and cylinder presses

The cylinder press uses a revolving cylinder to roll paper over the type or printing surface. The small cylinder press, intended for proofing type, is often called a proof press. With a proof press, the printing cycle is rarely powered. An inking system using rollers is usually part of the machine, and is often powered. The term "cylinder press" to a commercial printer means a large, powered machine for book or newspaper work, but among fine printers the term is also applied to a small hand-powered press.

A platen press uses a flat-faced platen to hold the paper and carry it toward a bed. On the bed, type is held in a frame or *chase*. The platen usually rocks from a near-horizontal position to a vertical one during the printing cycle. The paper is placed on the platen while it is horizontal, and the impression is made when the platen is vertical. On larger presses, the bed often rocks a short distance toward and away from the platen, allowing the platen room to rotate to a near-horizontal position.

Platen presses are powered by motor, hand, or foot. Some are small and are designed to be set up on a cabinet or table; larger presses have an integral stand. An inking system is almost always part of the machine, usually with a round disc on top serving as a reservoir for ink.

The hand press (shown in figure 1) is the most ancient of press designs, with a horizontal platen that is lowered toward a horizontal bed. It is operated with a lever that is drawn across the press. The bed typically slides out from under the platen for inking, and the paper is either laid directly on the type or is held on a hinged frame that is placed over the bed. As the name implies, they are powered only by hand; they are also known as common presses,

Washington proof presses, or Ben Franklin-style presses. An inking system is almost never part of the machine, and the inking is done by hand.

Throw-off

A throw-off slightly separates the bed and platen, or the bed and cylinder, so no impression is made while the press runs. On most presses, the form rollers continue to ink the type.

On platen presses with flywheels, either foot powered or motor driven, the throw-off allows the operator to step away from the press briefly, prevents the type from printing on the tympan when a sheet hasn't been fed, and allows the printer to save a sheet that has been misfed but not printed. If the tympan is accidentally printed on, the ink will transfer to the back of the next several sheets which are run through the press. The throw-off also allows the type to be inked without making an impression; printers sometimes use this feature to double-ink a heavy form for each impression.

On hand cylinder presses, the throw-off or *trip* allows the printer to apply extra ink to the type, a technique especially useful at the beginning of a run. On powered cylinder presses, the throw-off allows the printer to skip an impression when he or she isn't prepared to feed a sheet.

Makeready and impression

A press is made ready to print by applying the ink, setting up paper guides, and adjusting the pressure that the press will exert on the paper and type or plate. The process is known as *makeready*. A press which is inked and ready to print is ready, however, for only a particular kind and weight of paper: different papers require differing amounts of impression and ink for the same form.

The impression is adjusted to accommodate the different forms that will be printed, the different thicknesses of paper that will be used, and any variation in height within the form.

Too much pressure will soon wear out type, and too little will make a poor impression. The pressure is usually evaluated by inspecting the amount of embossing that is visible on the reverse side of the sheet.

Today, many letterpress printers intentionally generate an exaggerated amount of impression, producing a deep embossing and a noticeable, three-dimensional quality to the printing. These printers are often working with photopolymer plates, which are durable and disposable, rather than metal type.

Many commercial printers who formerly worked in letterpress will say, however, that "the type should kiss the paper." They were trained to print with the subtlest of impression in order to preserve the type.

The *American Dictionary of Printing and Bookmaking* of 1894 suggests that printers once took steps to *remove* the embossing from printed sheets. In the entry on the signature press, a device that compressed paper after printing, the *Dictionary* says: "paper . . . must be in a standing or hydrostatic press for a number of hours to efface the marks of impression."

Prior to 1800, printers used paper made of linen or cotton fiber and printed on it after it was dampened with water. With this method, a rich impression was obtained without injuring the type. This method remains the best means for obtaining fine, even printing on cotton and linen paper.

The tympan and packing

Platens and cylinders are covered with *packing*. *Tympan paper* is manufactured specifically for the outer surface of the packing, but any paper of reasonable hardness can be used. Many printers use mylar for the tympan because its surface is both firm and easy to clean when printed on. Sheets of heavy paper are placed under the tympan paper to form the packing. The packing should not be too soft, since this will wear the edges of the type.

The grain of the packing and tympan on a cylinder press should lie across the cylinder for best results. The tympan and packing must be replaced when worn.

Overlays

Overlays are isolated bits of packing that increase the pressure in a particular area. They are sometimes used for a line of type, or even an individual letter, which is worn and would otherwise plunge into the paper with insufficient force. They lie above the type, which gives rise to their name. Usually a very thin material is all that is needed, and cellophane tape, document repair tape, and tissue paper are commonly used. The overlay may be placed directly on the tympan, and held in place with tape or glue. They can be modified, if necessary, with sandpaper or a sharp knife. On cylinder presses, one edge of the material may be clamped into the grippers.

Overlays may also be placed within the packing itself. This is especially true on platen presses, since overlays placed on top of the tympan will generally interfere with feeding. A knife can be used to pierce the packing to show where the overlay should be placed.

Overlays within the packing may move out of position unless they are pasted down to a part of the packing that is held under a tympan bale. Tape can be used if it can be applied so that it is clear of the printing area.

Overlays can be forgotten in the packing when the press is made ready for the next project, possibly damaging type. When preparing a press for printing, always check for overlays placed for the last project by running a hand over the tympan, or by opening the packing and inspecting it.

With plates, and sometimes with type, pressure is adjusted by placing tape or paper *under* the plate or type, creating an *underlay*. Paper is usually glued to the plate. When a part of a plate must be raised to increase the impression in a small area, cut the pieces of paper needed for the underlay directly from a proof, which will show the exact sizes and shapes needed. Often, the outer edges of a block will create more pressure than other areas, and the impression will be balanced by an underlay that raises the inner portion of a block but not the edges.

A glue which dries and remains soft should be used in the packing. Some glues contain water, and may cause the bed, cylinder, or platen to rust as the glue dries. When using glue, talc can be rubbed over the overlay to absorb any excess.

Positioning the paper on the press

It is an art, rather than a science, to properly position the paper in relation to the type. I seldom bother to take a ruler to the press; the entire process can be done by eye.

When a proof is taken from the press, one can quickly see whether the printing is centered on the sheet by folding the proof in half and holding the sheet to the light. The fold is made perpendicular to the lines of type; the test will also show if the lines are square on the sheet. Note the amount of excess white space in the largest side margin of the sheet; to correct the imbalance, the position of the sheet must be moved half the amount of the excess, in the direction away from the excess.

The methods for adjusting the position of paper and type vary for cylinder and platen presses, and are described separately below.

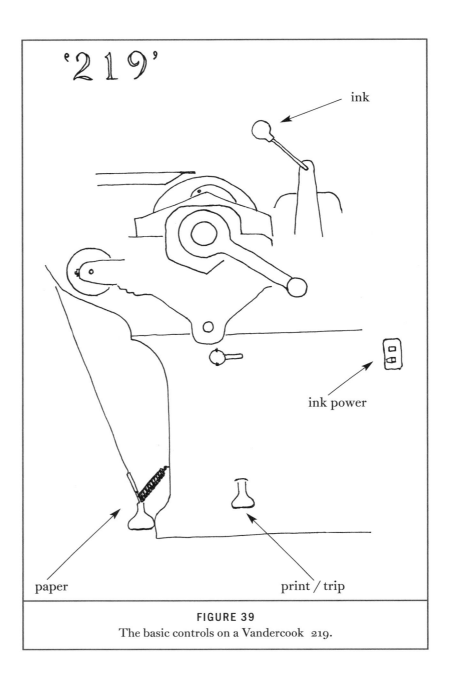

FIGURE 39
The basic controls on a Vandercook 219.

9

General Workings: Cylinder Press

A cylinder press holds type on a horizontal bed and paper on a cylinder, and the cylinder either rolls over the bed, or the bed rolls under the cylinder. There must be a means of lifting the cylinder away from the bed so that the press can return to its feed position; this is often done automatically. There were many variations produced, including drum cylinders, which are large, powered cylinder presses whose cylinder is twice as large as needed, with half the cylinder machined away to clear the bed as the bed returns. One popular commercial press, the Miehle Vertical, is a cylinder press with an upright bed. On large presses, the type is usually carried in a chase. On small presses, it is simply locked up against bars at the tail and head, and against the sides of the bed.

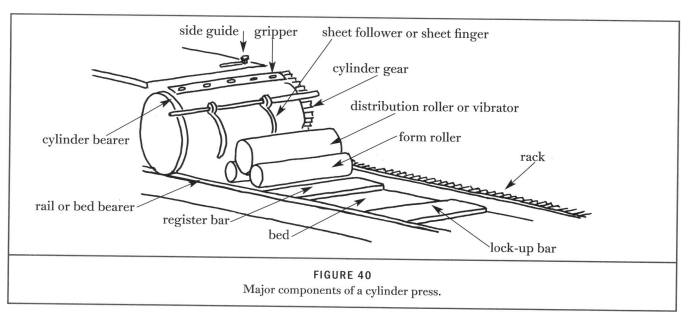

FIGURE 40
Major components of a cylinder press.

Deadline

Paper is held on a cylinder press with a series of clamps called grippers. Since these are mounted on the surface of the cylinder, there is no clearance between them and the type. Anything on the bed that is type high will be crushed if struck by the grippers.

The deadline is a line on the bed, either real or imaginary, which marks the boundary of the area in which paper grippers or other parts of the machine will strike and damage the printing surface when the press is operated.

On many presses, the deadline—the boundary of the grippers—is clear of the entire bed. On some presses, a steel piece of furniture called a *dead bar* or *register bar* lies at the head of the bed to hold the type clear of the deadline.

On other presses, the deadline is on the bed where type or other material might be placed. Such a deadline should *always* be marked on the bed of the press, preferably with red paint.

A press may have a deadline on the *tail end* of the bed. After making the impression, the cylinder may rotate until the grippers again pass over the bed. It is also possible that a press has two deadlines, one at the head and one at the tail.

When using an unfamiliar press, the printer must assume that the grippers will strike the type, especially near the head of the bed, until it is determined otherwise. One method is to set up the form with plenty of margin at the head of the press to ensure clearance, pull a proof, and then adjust the margin.

A more efficient method is to transfer a mark from the cylinder to the bed before any material is placed on the press. A mark is made on the bearing surface of the cylinder, in line with the trailing edge of the grippers, with a spot of paint or ink. The cylinder is turned over the entire length of the bed to transfer the paint to the bearing rail, revealing the position of the grippers in relation to the bed. On a Vandercook 219, a brass blade is positioned to wipe clean the bearing surface of the cylinder; on such a press, the cylinder may have to be turned backwards to transfer the mark.

If the mark shows that the grippers roll over the bed where type might be positioned, the mark should be transferred to the side of the bed at once, since the working of the press will soon wear away the mark on the face of the bearing rail. You may also mark the bed itself. A carpenter's square will help create a professional appearance that will prevent the deadline from being mistaken for a random mark. Red paint is traditional for a deadline.

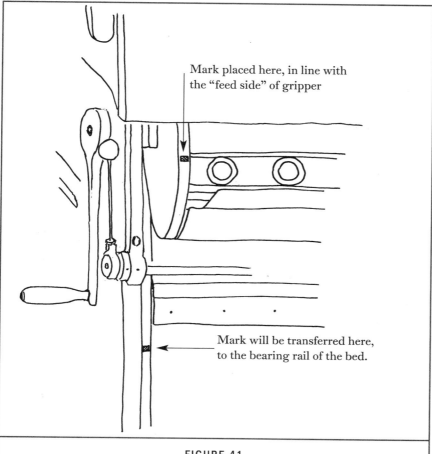

Mark placed here, in line with
the "feed side" of gripper

Mark will be transferred here,
to the bearing rail of the bed.

FIGURE 41
Marking deadline position.
When the grippers on a press will strike the type on the bed, the deadline,
which indicates the boundary of the grippers' range, should be marked on the
press. A paint mark, transferred from the cylinder bearer to the rail, is the most
accurate way of determining the position of the deadline.

It is usually possible to adjust a press so that the grippers clear the entire
bed. The adjustment requires lifting the cylinder clear of the gear track on
the side of the bed and (depending on the press) either rotating the cylinder
or moving the bed so that the two are re-timed in relation to each other. It
is also possible to replace the dead bar with one which covers the part of the
bed that can be struck by the grippers.

Avoid clutter on the feedboard and bed

Such things as tools, rulers, and pencils left on the feedboard of a cylinder press are liable to fall into the rollers or onto the bed of the press. They are also easily lost in the proofs and paper stock that accumulate there, and can be drawn with the paper into the press during printing. In either case, damage to the type is likely, and damage to the press is possible. After making the press ready to print, clear the feedboard of everything except paper.

It is likewise important to remove all tools from the *bed* of the press before operating it. Many small tools, such as quoin keys, are designed to lie below the printing plane when set directly on the bed, but it is easy to forget those that don't, or to place a tool on top of furniture, where it won't lie below the printing plane. Cultivate the habit of clearing all tools from the bed each time you operate the press.

Replacing the packing and tympan

When the tympan is embossed by too many impressions, it is replaced. The packing is usually replaced when the tympan is renewed.

The new tympan and packing must be cut to cover the cylinder surface without overlapping the bearing surfaces on each side of the cylinder, or the cylinder will be lifted away from the type. The old tympan and packing can be used as a pattern.

The surface of the cylinder is intentionally made with a smaller diameter than required for contact with the type. This *undercut* (the difference between the cylinder diameter and the diameter of the cylinder bearers) is filled with paper packing in order to increase the cylinder diameter and create an impression. Vandercooks typically have the amount of undercut stamped on the cylinder next to the bearers; for Vandercook and Challenge presses, .040″ is the usual amount of undercut. The cylinder packing is usually made about .003″ higher than the cylinder bearers to create the correct impression.

When I feel ambitious, I cut new tympan paper square on both ends with a lever paper cutter, or a T-square and knife or scissors. Then I score the ends with a blunt tool and T-square, so that the folds intended for the tympan clamp and take-up rod are square. This gives the best result. When I feel slovenly, I cut the ends square but avoid the scoring, forming a simple fold.

With the tympan clamped in place near the grippers, the press is moved forward until the packing can be inserted between the tympan and the cylinder. The press is then moved until the take-up rod can be reached. The end of the tympan is inserted into the slot in the take-up rod, or taped to the rod when no slot is provided, and the tympan is stretched first with the fingers and then lightly with a lever inserted into a hole in the take-up rod. The pawl on the rod's ratchet is engaged to maintain tension on the tympan. Draw the tympan tight, but don't allow it to tear.

After replacing the tympan, make certain that the tympan and packing don't cover the bearing surfaces on the sides of the cylinder. If they do, loosen the take-up rod and slide the packing clear.

Lubricating the cylinder press

Cylinder presses require frequent lubrication. The method is described in the chapter titled "Lubrication."

Inking

After oiling, feed the press a dab of ink. Apply the same amount of ink as you would honey to cover a piece of toast. Do not be a glutton, and remember that it is always easier to add ink than remove it.

Wiping the ink across the uppermost roller, from right to left, is probably the best way to distribute ink evenly; on some presses, other rollers will be more accessible. The ink is fully distributed by running the ink system. Watch for any obvious problems, such as a roller which is carrying too much ink on one side. Vandercook operators should form the habit of lowering the form rollers onto the ink drum only when the motor is turning; this practice reduces strain on the chain linking the motor and drum.

More information on adjusting ink and rollers is in the chapter titled "Ink and rollers."

While the ink is being spread over all of the ink-carrying surfaces, the grippers and end guides can be adjusted, and when the ink is well-distributed, the first proof can be made.

Preparing the grippers and end guides

Paper is more likely to be carried squarely on the press when it is held by a number of grippers, rather than a few. When possible, arrange the form so that the sheet is fed with its longest edge into the grippers, especially when sheets are small.

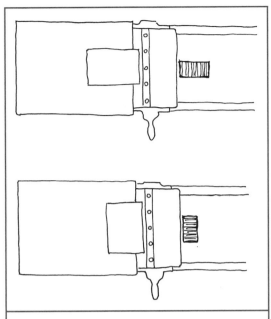

FIGURE 42
Orienting paper on the press.
Use as many grippers as possible on a cylinder
press, in order to keep the sheet more squarely
on the press. The bottom arrangement is usually preferable in terms of paper feeding.

Paper will bend more neatly around the cylinder when the paper's grain direction lies across the cylinder, and with heavy papers it may be necessary to feed them accordingly.

Ideally, the block of type can be positioned with roughly equal space between the block and each rail or side, but type will print successfully anywhere on the press. Small blocks of type must often be positioned near the side of the bed in order to make the side guide useable—the correct position depends on the size of the sheet and its margins. Everything should be positioned on the bed so that the side guide can be adjusted in both directions while the press is prepared for printing. At first, the paper position need only be approximate, with crude corrections of the side guide.

During repositioning, the side guide is liable to move abruptly, so that all indication of both the original position and the hoped-for position are lost. Avoid this by holding a sheet firmly against the feedboard with one hand to mark either the original or the desired position, while adjusting the side guide with the other hand.

As proofs are made and the position of the sheet approaches the ideal place, minute adjustments of the side guide can be made with the fine screw only, while the guide itself remains locked in place.

Many cylinder presses have adjustable end guides that can be used to alter the angle at which the sheets are held on the cylinder, and to make minute adjustments to the starting position of the sheet. These are usually located between the grippers, and can be set either to interact with the sheet or to be backed off out of the way. It is best to back all of these off when preparing the press, using only the grippers to orient the sheet. If the end guides are needed to cock the sheet or hold it away from the grippers, only two, near the corners of the sheet, should be used.

With the printer's free hand, the sheet can be held back tightly against the tympan as the cylinder rotates to make the impression. This is useless with a short sheet, which must be released before the impression begins. The practice can be dangerous, as the hand is liable to be drawn in too far and wedged between the cylinder and some part of the press. Evaluate the work, and see if holding the sheet is accomplishing anything. Make a practice of releasing the sheet before your hand is drawn past the top of the cylinder.

Adjusting the sheet fingers and feed table

Sheet fingers are used to hold the sheet against the cylinder, or, in some designs, simply to prevent the sheet from falling against the ink rollers. Many printers pay no attention to them until they are needed to correct a problem, such as slurring of the type or soiling from the press. On many presses, they will strike the type if allowed to hang too far down, and care must be taken whenever adjusting them.

The final adjustment to the press is the positioning of the feed table, a refinement that sometimes allows the sheets to slide into the grippers more consistently. On a Challenge style press with a moving bed, this adjustment is often needed for taking the sheets off the press. When the tail of a long sheet ends up on the feed table side of the cylinder, room must be provided between the table and the cylinder so that it can be reached.

The sheet can be taken off the cylinder only when the cylinder comes to a position at which the sheet can be grasped. On some presses, the grippers release automatically at the end of the bed's travel, and on many, the cylinder is lifted into the *trip* or non-printing position for the return. Vandercooks are said to benefit, mechanically, from a complete run to the end of the bed; some can be set for a short pass.

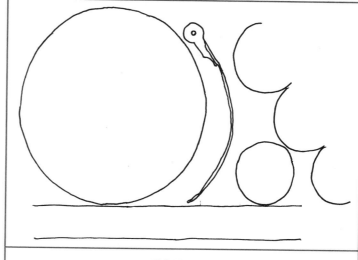

FIGURE 43
Adjusting sheet fingers.
On some cylinder presses, the sheet fingers will strike the form if not properly positioned. Use care whenever adjustments are made.

Adjusting the press for impression

On a cylinder press, the adjustment in impression is made by adding and removing paper. The cylinder—which is made slightly smaller in diameter than needed for contact with the type—is packed with paper or other material to increase its circumference and serve as a means of adjustment. The printer doesn't adjust the impression mechanically. The bearing surfaces on the sides of the cylinder always rest on the bearing rails of the bed, making the distance between the bed and the cylinder surface fixed.

The impression *balance*, so critical on a platen press, is not a concern on a cylinder press. This is because the overall pressure generated on a cylinder press is limited by the minute area of contact between the type and the press cylinder. The parts of the press are not deflected enough to affect the impression. And less radical adjustment is needed for a cylinder press because it isn't expected to handle very heavy stock, since heavy stock can't bend sufficiently around the cylinder. For these two reasons, the distance between the bed and the cylinder surface isn't routinely adjusted on a cylinder press. It can, however, be adjusted to correct problems that develop as the press surfaces wear.

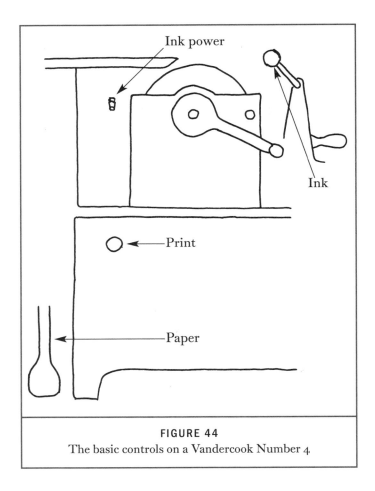

FIGURE 44
The basic controls on a Vandercook Number 4.

10

General Workings: Platen Press

A platen press holds type in a chase which is mounted vertically on the press. The platen, which holds the paper, usually rotates to a near-horizontal position for the feeding and take-off of paper, and rotates to a vertical position for impression. On floor models, the bed normally rocks toward the platen as the platen rotates. The impression is made when the bed and platen are parallel.

There are many variations on this process. The most common variant is a fixed bed, which doesn't move toward the platen, and requires that the platen make all of the movement to close the press.

Platen lock

Many platen presses have a mechanism for locking the platen in a rigid position while the impression is made. On a C&P full-sized press, for example, the platen is mounted on a *rocker* that rotates the platen to a vertical position. When the platen is in position for the impression, an extension of the rocker comes to rest against the frame. Then, a *rocker lock* swings forward to lock the bottom of the rocker extension, and the platen is rigidly held.

Grippers and gauge pins must be clear of the type

The first rule of operating a platen press is never to mount a chase and close the press without checking that grippers and gauge pins are clear of the type. This vigilance must extend throughout the press run, first because the position of the type within the chase may be altered when corrections are made, and second because it is possible to replace the chase in the press upside down, thus putting the type in harm's way.

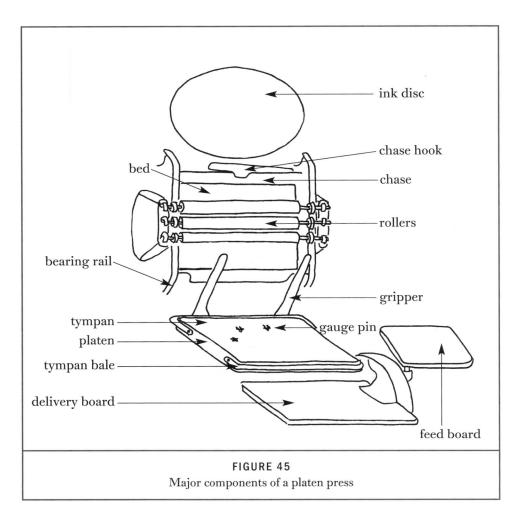

FIGURE 45
Major components of a platen press

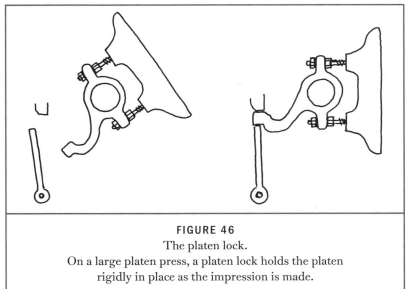

FIGURE 46
The platen lock.
On a large platen press, a platen lock holds the platen
rigidly in place as the impression is made.

Tympan bales

Any time the tympan bales are opened to alter the tympan or packing, there is danger that the press will subsequently be closed with one or both bales lying open. Even without a form on the press, there isn't clearance for open tympan bales between the bearing rails and the tympan. If the press is closed with a tympan bale open, the bale will likely be broken off and the platen surface damaged.

As a rule, never leave the press for more than a moment when the bales are open; if called away, close the bales before leaving the press. Make it a habit, after stopping the press for an extended time, to check that the bales are closed before restarting.

Lubricating the platen press

Platen presses require lubrication at least daily; the method is described in the chapter titled "Lubrication."

Inking

After oiling, feed the press a dab of ink on the disk. For a table-top press, apply the same amount of ink as you would honey to cover half a piece of toast. For a floor-model platen press, use enough to cover an entire piece of toast. Do not be a glutton, and remember that it is always easier to add ink than remove it.

With a platen press, the ink is distributed by running the press. Because most platen presses have no means of holding the rollers off of the type, the press must be charged with ink, and the ink distributed over the ink disk, before the form is placed on the press. Otherwise, the type would be inundated with excess ink as the press works to distribute the ink over the disk.

Many printers are comfortable adding additional ink to the press while it is running, while others feel it is safe to add ink only when a press is stopped. In either case, the ink is added to the lower corner of the ink disk so that it will be rolled out as many times as possible before the rollers carry it over the type. On a C&P full-sized press or a C&P Pilot, for example, where the ink disk rotates clockwise, the ink is added to the lower left corner of the disk.

More information on adjusting ink and rollers is in the chapter titled "Ink and rollers."

When the ink is evenly distributed on all surfaces, the chase can be

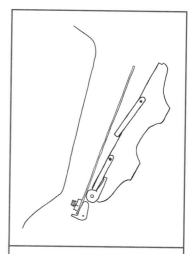

FIGURE 47
Ensure that bales are closed! To avoid disaster, tympan bales on a platen press must be closed before the bed and platen are brought together.

mounted and the first proof made. First, however, the packing should be checked for overlays.

Checking the tympan packing

The tympan packing should be checked for overlays that have been placed within it, since these may damage the type. The inspection can be done by carefully feeling the packing; a more thorough investigation is made by opening one of the bales and lifting the tympan and packing.

If the tympan is in poor condition, embossed by too many forms or roughened by too many gauge pins, it should be replaced.

Replacing the packing and tympan

When replacing the tympan, it is usually necessary to replace the packing beneath it. Stretch the tympan as tightly as possible. To avoid frequent changes of the tympan, I try to print small blocks of type near the bottom of a fresh tympan, and work my way up toward the top with each new project.

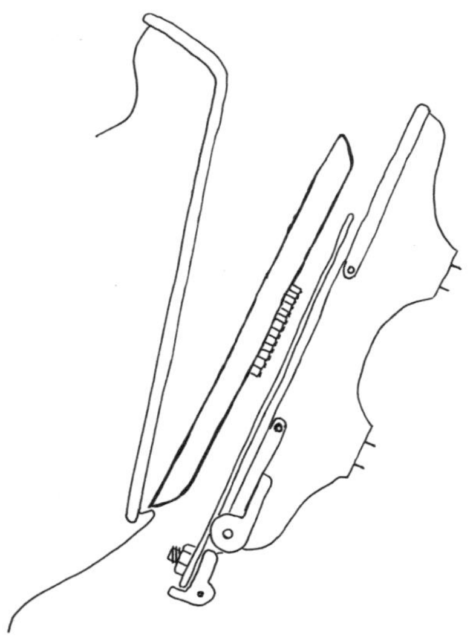

Mounting the chase

When the packing is ready, the chase and the form within it are placed into the press. On large presses, the chase is lowered into the press while being held at the top. The printer may stand in front of the press or on the side.

When mounting the chase from the side, the press is opened fully and the rollers are at the bottom of the bed.

When mounting the chase from the front, the press is nearly closed, and the rollers are on the lower portion of the ink disk. It may be helpful to rotate the flywheel enough to move the rollers up the ink disk in order to work the clamp without contacting the rollers and soiling the hands, and mount the chase on the bottom flanges. Then, holding the top of the chase back against the outside of the chase clamp with one hand, rotate the flywheel with the other hand to close the press and bring the clamp closer to you. When removing the chase, open the press so that the chase can be lifted without striking the grippers.

It takes practice to properly lower the chase onto the flanges that support it on the bottom of the bed; it's rather easy to miss one or

FIGURE 48
The type will be damaged if it strikes the grippers or tympan when the chase is lowered into or lifted from a platen press.

both. The chase should be lowered into the press about two thirds of the way, and then, with the lower edge of the chase held against the bed, the chase should be slid squarely down the bed to the flanges. The novice should practice a few times with an empty chase.

The chase is positioned against the left side of the bed by convention. This ensures that it is mounted on the press in the same position after being taken from the press for corrections or cleaning. Once in position, a clamp holds the chase in place.

With the press inked and the form mounted on the press, make an impression directly on the tympan. Again, close the press carefully to ensure that no contact is made between the type and the grippers. By closing the press slowly and by hand, one can feel how much impression force is developed by the press, and can reverse the action if the pressure seems excessive.

The ink which now lies on the tympan is dried with talcum powder, a small amount of which is rubbed about by hand.

Positioning gauge pins

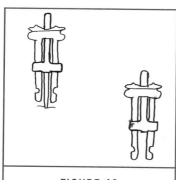

FIGURE 49
Gauge pins are stabbed into the tympan about a quarter of an inch away from the desired position of the sheet edge.

With the type printed on the tympan, finding the correct position for the gauge pins is straightforward. If the form has lines of type, rule, or art that prints horizontally on the tympan, one can measure away from the line to make a parallel line on which to position the gauge pins at the bottom of the tympan. One can also cut or fold a piece of heavy paper to the proper size and place one edge along one of the printed lines or rules so that the other edge reveals the position of the pins; if the lines lie vertically on the tympan, a square piece of paper will show where the line of gauge pins should be placed. But a useful method for most jobs is to get the pins close to their positions by eye and then adjust them after proofing. Since the form is usually square in relation to the tympan, the sheet can be positioned by eye-balling the margins of the tympan around it.

Gauge pins must be placed far enough away from the type block so that their tongues also stay clear of the type.

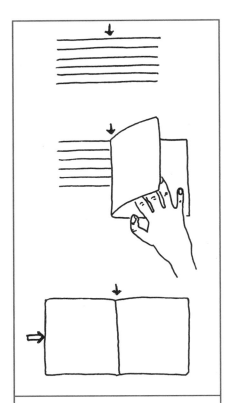

FIGURE 50
Positioning paper on a platen press
is best done after an impression is
printed directly on the tympan.
If the center of the printed image is
found and marked (top), the center
of a folded sheet can be positioned
there (center). When the sheet is
opened (bottom), the position of the
left edge will be revealed.

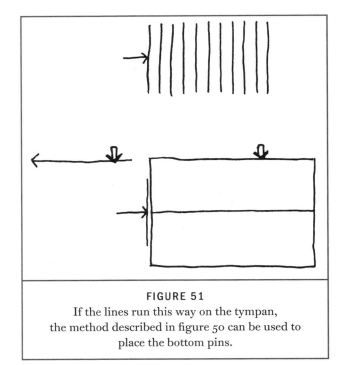

FIGURE 51
If the lines run this way on the tympan,
the method described in figure 50 can be used to
place the bottom pins.

Since the grippers will damage the gauge pins if they lie over them when the press is closed, pay attention to the ideal position for the grippers when placing the gauge pins. The grippers must lie over the margins of the sheet, so the gauge pins at the bottom of the tympan must be placed between the grippers, away from the margins of the sheet.

The gauge pins are stabbed through the tympan paper, proofs are made, and the pins are brought to their final positions. For efficiency in feeding and for consistency in registration, it's important to make the pins square with one another.

When all is right, the pins are tapped lightly with a quoin key and their feet are driven down into the packing to set them in position. Once driven down, the pins can be further stabilized with tape or a hard wax such as sealing wax which is melted onto both the tympan and the body of the pin. But before doing any setting of the pins, take a couple of proofs to be certain that the pins are correctly positioned.

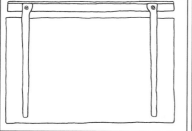 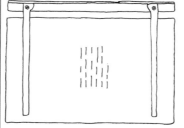

After any previously-used gauge pins and overlays have been removed from the tympan and packing, the grippers are moved to the sides (left). An impression is made directly on the tympan (right).

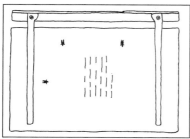 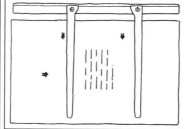

The gauge pins are set (left), leaving room for the grippers to be positioned over the margins of the sheet (right).

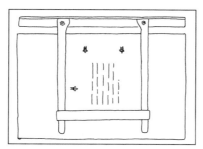

If margins are not adequate for the grippers to lie between the gauge pins and type block, a rubber band can be stretched between the grippers.

FIGURE 52
Positioning gauge pins and grippers on a platen press

The tongues of the gauge pins should be set so that they grip the paper that is fed, but they should not be so far out from the body of the gauge pin that it is difficult to slide the paper beneath them. The tongues can be bent slightly so that they lie at the proper height above the tympan.

It is possible to print on a sheet that is larger than the platen by improvising sheet holders which extend beyond the edges. These are usually simple fingers of light cardboard glued or taped to the tympan and folded to hold the paper edge. On a 10 × 15 C&P, the total available clearance for paper is about 22 inches in width. Only about two additional inches are available below the platen.

Positioning the grippers

The grippers hold the sheet against the tympan while the press closes, while the impression is made, and while the press opens and the type separates from the sheet. If a gripper or an attached finger contacts a gauge pin when the press closes, it will crush it. If a gripper or an attached finger contacts the printing surface of the type, it will crush the type. The grippers must therefore be placed to clear both the gauge pins and the type. As the final step in makeready, the grippers (or their attached fingers) are moved into position over the margins of the sheet and secured.

This can be problematic when the margins are small. When there is no room for the grippers themselves, however, a heavy rubber band or two can usually be stretched between them. Rubber bands are easy to set up, and they stay in place; anything which wandered over the type would, of course, be disastrous. Rubber bands in large sizes are available from office supply stores.

Adjusting the press for impression

On a platen press, the overall pressure is normally adjusted with paper packing placed below the tympan. The balance or distribution of the pressure is adjusted with impression screws, which are positioned near each corner of the platen and increase or decrease the space between the platen and the bed in that area. Adjustment for balance is necessary on a platen press because different forms, in different positions on the press, absorb the force of the impression differently and affect the relative positions of the bed and the platen as the press closes.

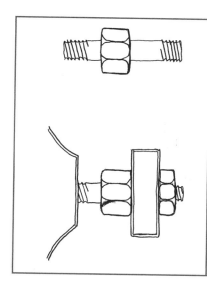

FIGURE 53
Platen press impression screw. An impression screw is typically one piece (top). When mounted on the press (bottom), the impression is adjusted by rotating the screw with the large nut-like flange in the center. A nut (at right) locks the impression screw in place on the press, and must be loosened before any adjustments are made.

Running the platen press

When all is ready, a powered press is run at a pace which is moderate enough so that the printer can position each sheet onto the gauge pins without missing a cycle. This is especially important for presses without a throw-off, since a missed sheet will mean an impression on the tympan which must be dried with talc, costing time. But even with a throw-off, a job printed at a rapid pace, with a sheet missed once every ten cycles, will require the same time when run at 90 percent of that pace with each sheet printed.

The paper is picked up from the feed table with the right hand and placed onto the bottom gauge pins about an inch from the side gauge pin, then slid against the side pin. After the impression is made, the left hand removes the printed piece from the tympan and piles it on the delivery board. In the interval between cycles, inspect each piece for soil, crooked impression, workups, and slurring. Examine the back of an occasional sheet for set-off from the tympan. Discard defective sheets directly onto the floor.

Various things can be applied to the printer's fingers to make them grip the stock, which is especially helpful when taking off the printed sheets. Sandpaper, rubber finger caps, and glycerin are traditional. I prefer spittle. The hands should be washed clean before feeding stock; a section on hand washing appears on page 132.

Safety

Machine platen presses cause severe injury when the operator allows his or her hand to be drawn into the rollers or to be pinched between the platen and bed. Once the press begins to close, the hands should be habitually drawn away from the tympan. Prepare yourself mentally so that you never attempt to grasp a sheet that is misfed or that becomes displaced on the press. There is additional information on machinery in the chapter on safety.

Runaway sheets on the platen press

Occasionally, a sheet will be pulled away from the tympan by the adhesion of the ink on the type and then be caught by the rollers, which will wrap the sheet around themselves and carry the sheet to the ink disk. The press is stopped and the sheet, which will now be saturated with ink, should be removed with a pliers as the flywheel is turned to rotate the rollers. The grippers should be adjusted or enhanced to avoid a repetition.

11

Troubleshooting the Printed Image

A guide to correcting press problems

Fuzzy image Type is over-inked; type, form or paper is moving during printing; paper is creating lint. Check type and form for movement in chase or on bed; check packing for rigidity and stability. Check grippers on a platen press, check press for excessive mechanical play. Check ink for lint.

Slurred image Type, form, or paper is moving during printing. Check type and form for movement in chase or on bed; check packing for rigidity and stability. Check grippers on a platen press, check press for excessive mechanical play. Check ink tackiness: too tacky an ink may cause the paper to be dragged across type at separation. Apply frisket. With enclosed borders, air may be compressed in border; drill holes in border to allow air to escape. Check height of plates or type, and thickness of cylinder packing.

Light image Press is developing too little impression, or ink is too light. Always experiment with increased impression before adding ink.

Uneven image Type is poorly planed. Material is caught under type. Type is poorly inked because of poor roller condition, poor roller adjustment, improper roller speed, or poor ink distribution between distributor and form rollers. Added ink not rolled out sufficiently. Impression balance needs adjustment on a platen press. Overlays or underlays need adjustment; packing is dented. When parts of some letters are faint: type off its feet (meaning feet were not squarely on imposing surface when type was planed, or type was lifted in form); part of type is lifting when locked up; type battered or worn. If printing on dampened paper, paper may not be evenly

FIGURE 54

A proof from type which is "off its feet." Type which is not properly planed will sometimes stand at a slight angle, or off its feet, creating the characteristic shading effect seen here, particularly in the final group of 'e's.

dampened. On a Kelsey with removable bed, ensure that the bed and chase are mounted on the press correctly.

Parts of letters faint Poor contact between ink roller and type; type off its feet (meaning feet were not squarely on imposing surface when form was planed, or type was lifted in form); inadequate impression; worn type. Check for faults in "Uneven image," above.

Spaces print Correct the lock-up, checking for even pressure on block of type. Check for anomalies that prevent even pressure across block, such as long leads, warped furniture, and oversized spacing or type. See section in text on workups.

Furniture prints Inspect lock-up for loose or lifted furniture. Ensure that ink rollers are properly set. On a platen press, ensure that impression is properly balanced. Ensure that sheet is properly held by grippers on a platen press.

Leads, slugs print Ensure that form is tight; ensure that type-high rule has not inadvertently been substituted for slugs and leads.

Image shifts Check gauge pins for stability on platen press; maintain constant speed on motorized press; check adhesive bond when using polymer plates with adhesives; add adhesive on magnetic base. Be careful when opening form to ensure proper repositioning of furniture and spacing; place quoins properly in relation to feed guides and grippers (on a cylinder press) and gauge pins (on a platen press).

Soiling from press Check position of sheet fingers (on a cylinder press), and grippers (on a platen press). Enhance platen press grippers with rubber bands, etc. if necessary. Check paper side of grippers for soil. As last resort, make a frisket to mask the sheet, or tape tail of each sheet to tympan on a cylinder press.

12

Printing Presses

Description

Presses are usually designated by their maker, type or model, and size. Platen presses are usually sized according to the capacity of their chase in inches, while cylinder presses are sized by the capacity of their bed. A platen press might be described as "a C&P 10 × 15 old style." A cylinder press might be described as "a Vandercook number 4" or "a Challenge 20 × 26." It is not always clear what the limits of a bed are when working with measurements used to size a cylinder press. Some manufacturers measure between the rails, and others measure the rather arbitrary "useable size of the bed." Some measurements comprise the length of the bed from dead bar to lock-up bar, and others include the whole bed.

Choosing a press: generalities

Novice printers should first decide if they are artists or printers, and if they will be producing their work in editions of tens or hundreds. They should also consider the form or size of what they will be printing.

The overall size and weight of the press itself is often important. Though the hand cylinder press is a comparatively compact machine for the printing capacity, there is no satisfactory small or lightweight version of it, but there are many good platen presses which are small and light, with some designed to occupy a table top. There are also small treadle-powered platens, such as the Pearl, that can easily be moved into cramped quarters.

With most platen presses, the construction isn't heavy enough to print a form which fills the entire chase with type without stressing the press, rather, they are designed to print a form that uses, say, no more than half the chase's capacity.

If a press was once popular, advice and parts can be located more easily. But the condition of a press is more important than its popularity, and an obscure but little-used press in fine condition is preferable to a more popular press that is worn or is in need of restorative work.

Choosing a press: the hand cylinder press

The hand cylinder press is a good choice for the artist who will be printing wood engravings, wood or linoleum cuts, and large plates or forms of type. Because the cylinder press prints only a small portion of the form at a time, this kind of press can handily print large cuts and type that would require enormous pressure and carefully balanced impression if printed with the single stroke of a platen. And because of the small area of contact, the beds can be relatively large, so the press can handle a large sheet of paper.

The hand cylinder also offers several advantages for fine printing. First, its precise machining contributes to consistent impression with a minimum of makeready. Second, a stop in the work occurs after each sheet is printed, creating as much time as needed for the printer to check the result before printing the next sheet. Finally, the large format of the cylinder press allows the printer to lay out multiple pages, simplifying both the printing and binding process for printers interested in producing books. The large format also allows posters or broadsides to be printed.

In general, avoid a proof press that does not include both an inking system and a means of clamping the paper to the cylinder. While inking by hand seems like something that should be easily mastered, a hand-held brayer cannot apply the ink as consistently or evenly as machine-mounted systems. A system of grippers that steadfastly holds the paper to the cylinder while the impression is made is also important, both for quality and consistency.

Excellent proof presses are the Vandercook and the Challenge GP and K series.

Choosing a press: the platen press

For the printer who is planning to confine their work to smaller sizes, the platen press is a good choice. Once mastered, it will produce excellent work. For large editions, say of 200 or more, the platen press is less tedious to work than other kinds of presses. A *machine* version with a flywheel, whether driven by foot treadle or electric motor, is preferable for editions of more than a few hundred.

A hand-powered version has the advantage of providing an automatic stop in the printing which allows the printer to check for and correct problems. This advantage is usually of less importance, however, with the small formats printed on platen presses, because the operator of a powered press can check for problems while the next sheet is being printed. With a large or complicated form which cannot be completely scanned during the printing cycle, the printer can check progressive portions of the sheet each time.

In general, excellent platen presses are the Sigwalt, the Kelsey, the Chandler and Price Pilot, the medium and large Chandler and Price models, the Golding Pearl, the Colt's Armory, and the Heidelberg Windmill. The novice should avoid machines that incorporate automatic paper feeders, such as the Kluge or Heidelberg Windmill, as the feeders add a considerable degree of complexity.

Inspecting for purchase

When inspecting a press before purchase, the quantity and quality of the light available will make all of the difference in what you see and don't see. Bring your own trouble light or powerful flashlight.

First, survey the press carefully for broken or missing parts. With a platen press, look for the chase, rollers, roller trucks, grippers, treadle, and the gear system that rotates the ink disc, as these parts are the ones most likely to be missing. With a cylinder press, look for the end guides, lock-up bar, and sheet fingers. Parts such as these may have been removed from the press but may still be on the premises, and a little searching will sometimes turn them up.

On all presses, look for cam followers that are stuck in place and badly worn. Any repaired parts should be inspected for the quality of the repair. A professional weld in cast iron, for example, is perfectly serviceable, provided that the part has been properly re-aligned before welding.

Note carefully the condition of the oil holes. If they are filled with dirt, they were clearly not used regularly, and the bearing surfaces may be worn.

When inspecting a platen press, take hold of the bed and wrestle with it; the resulting play or movement should be very small. Do the same with the platen and side arms. Note the smoothness of the movement, especially in the bed, as the press opens and closes; watch for any sudden or erratic motion. Remove the tympan and inspect the surface of the platen for indentations, gouges or cracks; the platen should be relatively smooth, and its condition will often tell you a great deal about how the press has been used. Place a steel ruler or other straight edge on the bed and platen to determine

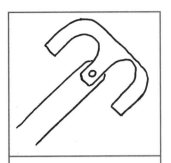

FIGURE 55
A worn roller saddle
on a platen press.

if they are warped or badly worn. Check the ink roller saddles for excessive wear. Check the condition of the impression screws by rotating them a bit. If the press has a mechanism for stabilizing the platen before impression, bring the press to the impression position, and check the platen lock and platen for play.

When inspecting a hand cylinder press, check the condition of the bed and cylinder. Remove the cylinder packing to inspect the cylinder. Inspect the gear track and rails for wear.

With any press, print with it before purchase, if possible.

Remember that many small parts can be re-manufactured or salvaged from another press. A machine shop can re-machine many metal surfaces. Rollers in poor condition can easily be re-cast; in some cases the original roller *cores* or steel shafts are re-used by the recaster, while in other cases new shafts are provided. Roller trucks for platen presses are easily purchased or made for many models; for other presses they aren't available for purchase and are difficult and expensive to machine.

Motors and shop power

A large press, either cylinder or platen, will usually be equipped with an electric motor. On a hand cylinder press, the motor simply powers the system that distributes ink and is relatively small. On other kinds of presses, the motor creates all of the motion required to run the press. If the press is one with continuous motion, such as a platen press or large cylinder press, there should be a means of adjusting the press's speed: the motor should be fitted with some kind of speed control.

When inspecting a press, make sure you survey its electrical specifications: the motor's requirements for form, voltage, frequency and phase must match those supplied by your shop wiring.

Motors on small presses normally run on *household current:* single phase, alternating current at 110 volts. Motors on large equipment may run on single phase 220 volts, or three-phase 220 volts. Older motors may be designed for forms of power that are now obsolete, such as direct current, two-phase, or a frequency of 50 cycles.

Electrical equipment is invariably marked with rating information on a plate or label; for most presses, a small plate is mounted on the motor. The plate normally shows ratings for horsepower, speed, voltage, form, phase, frequency, and amperage. If an electrical control box or speed control is part of the machine, look to that for information on the kind of current needed.

Speed refers to the speed of the motor shaft, and is usually stated in rotations per minute, or RPM. When a motor has adjustable speed, the rating will show a range, such as "50–150 RPM." The motor's speed is controlled by a separate electrical control box, or, with older motors, by a small lever protruding from the motor housing.

Voltage refers to the amount of potential or "pressure" in the current. Electric motors may safely be run with a voltage within ten percent of that specified on the motor. In North America, *household current* is variously described as 110, 115, and 120 volts, but 220 volts is also widely available in homes and shops. Some motors can be wired either for 110 or 220 volts by simple modification of the connections in the box mounted near the motor. The plate will show "110/220 volts," and the amperage will show two ratings as well. A wiring diagram on the motor or in the connecting box will show how the motor is to be wired for the two different voltages.

Form or type of current will be alternating or direct, usually indicated on the motor plate as "A.C." or "D.C." The speed of direct current motors is simple to control, so they are often used in combination with a control box that converts A.C. to D.C. In the nineteenth century, some areas were supplied with D.C. current, but A.C. is now universal for grid power.

Phase refers to the number of separate electrical currents used by the motor. Phase is usually shown on motor labels as "1" or "3," signifying single phase, or three-phase; the indication for phase may be "PH" or "φ." Three-phase motors really incorporate three motor circuits in one case, with each circuit's voltage timed or *phased* to peak sequentially, providing marked advantages in efficiency and starting. Three-phase current isn't generally available outside of commercial and industrial areas, but can be manufactured on site with a converter.

Frequency refers to the number of waves or cycles in one second. Sixty cycles per second (or sixty *hertz*) is standard in Canada, the U.S., and Central and Latin American. On motor plates, frequency in cycles per second is sometimes shown as "cycles," or "HZ" for hertz.

Amperage or amps refers to the amount of overall power required. The fuses or circuit breakers in distribution panels are rated in amps, and those controlling the circuit on which the motor will run must be adequate to power it. Motors will normally draw at least twice the rated number of amps when starting. Electrical codes call for a motor circuit that is two and one half times the amperage rating of the motor.

An electrical motor shop will be quite helpful when you face a problem with compatibility, and should be consulted for advice about selecting and installing a phase converter. A motor shop can also test a motor for condition.

On a press with an external motor—that is, one without a specialized housing or shaft that integrates the motor and machine—it should be quite simple to exchange the motor for one that includes a speed control or matches your shop's electrical characteristics.

For a platen press that is 10 × 15 or smaller it is also possible to convert to foot-power, adding an element of simplicity to its operation. Most platen presses are equipped with a shaft that contains a crook for a treadle, and a treadle is easy to install. New treadles for C&P's were still being sold by Hern Iron Works of Coeur d'Alene, Idaho, when this was written.

The flywheel of a platen press usually turns so that the top moves toward the back. A 10 × 15 platen press can be driven with a half horsepower motor. Information on electrical wiring appears in the chapter titled "The letterpress studio or shop."

Cylinder presses: hand cylinders

Small hand cylinder presses were designed as proof presses. The *galley proof press* is designed so that type can be left on galleys while printing, with additional clearance between the cylinder and bed to accommodate the thickness of the galley beneath the type. A galley plate, which can be placed on the bed to substitute for the galley's thickness, was often sold with the press; if this is missing, one is easily made from .050″ thick steel. With a galley plate, type can be placed directly on the press, rather than on a galley. A few presses have adjustable beds, so both type per se, and type on galleys, can be printed. Most hand cylinder presses, however, are *type high;* they are made to print from type standing with its feet directly on the bed.

There are four classes of proof presses:

> The ROLLING PIN STYLE of proof press has the cylinder rolling over rails on either side of the bed, with the printer rolling the cylinder's handles in his or her hands like a rolling pin.
> The SIGN PRESS STYLE has the cylinder mounted within a carriage, which is pulled by hand over the bed, guided by narrow rollers or wheels on rails. Presses made in the rolling pin and sign press styles are sometimes called *gravity presses.*
> The VANDERCOOK STYLE moves the cylinder over the bed on a geared track; the cylinder is rotated with a crank or motor.
> The CHALLENGE STYLE moves the bed under the cylinder, in the manner of a large cylinder press; the cylinder is rotated with a crank.

The rolling pin style proof press comes to us from the nineteenth century. Often beautifully styled, this kind of press lacks an inking system and a system for holding the paper on the cylinder.

The sign press style, designed to produce placards for retail stores, seldom includes an inking system. Many sign presses hold the paper stock in a clamp on the bed, but the limited diameter of their cylinder produces a poor impression. Several companies made this kind of machine, including Challenge, Vandercook, Line-o-Scribe, Morgan, and Show Card.

The proof press of the nineteenth century was designed to proof type, to create a crude but readable copy of text that could be checked for errors and used for elementary adjustments to layouts. Prior to its introduction, proofs were made with hand presses, or with hand-held, felt-covered planers that were laid over the proof paper and lightly tapped with a mallet. The nineteenth century proof press was an improvement on the proofing planer, but it lacked both an inking system and a gripper system for holding the stock on the cylinder—two important components for precise printing.

The twentieth century proof press was more refined. It was designed to make proofs that would show any defects in type or plates. Later in the century, it was used to create impeccable proofs from which lithographic plates could be made. Fine printers, who had generally used hand presses, began using cylinder presses for edition printing in the 1950s.

Twentieth century proof presses are carefully machined and capable of extremely fine reproduction. Most were designed for runs of perhaps one to three copies, since a powered press—whether lithographic or letterpress—would have been available for production in the typical commercial shop. As a result, twentieth century proof presses are easy to lock up, incorporate sophisticated inking systems, and are quickly adjusted for impression and inking, but they are cumbersome for long runs. Occasionally, one sees a press with automatic paper takeoff, and/or a motor which drives the cylinder through the printing cycle.

In the twentieth century, the proof press market was dominated by the Vandercook company of Chicago. But many manufacturers were active, including Replex, Asbern, Challenge, Canuck, Potter, Bower, and Hacker.

The machine or powered cylinder press

Printers who must produce high volumes and large formats often make use of the powered cylinder press, a large press designed to produce books and newspapers commercially. There were many, many makers of these presses, including Babcock, Chandler and Price, Heidelberg, Kelly, Miller, Miehle, and Challenge. A speed control and a throw-off are two important features.

All of the large cylinder presses slide the bed from one end of the press to the other while the cylinder spins and makes the impression. During the return of the bed, the cylinder must be lifted so that the form does not print on the tympan. If the cylinder stops when lifted, the press is called a *stop cylinder;* if it continues to spin while the bed returns, it is called a *two-revolution* press. A *drum cylinder* press, however, uses a large cylinder that is not lifted away from the bed; instead, the cylinder is twice the diameter needed for printing, and half of the surface of the cylinder is reduced in size to prevent contact between the form and cylinder as the bed returns.

Generally, a better-quality press has more than two form rollers, and uses a table as an ink reservoir. These presses incorporate either a fly system, which turns the sheet onto its printed side as it is delivered, or a face-up system, which uses fabric tapes to deliver the sheet. When contemplating the purchase of a large press, remember that they require correspondingly large areas for paper handling, composing, stonework and galley storage.

The platen press

The platen was designed for *job work,* or small commercial printing projects. Before the invention of this style of press in about 1840, job work was relatively rare. George Phineas Gordon, who is credited with many of the innovations now seen in the common platen press, reportedly said that his design for the rotating platen came to him from Ben Franklin, who appeared in a dream. Gordon later improved his design by mounting the bed on long feet that rocked it away from and toward the platen. Most large platen presses in use today can be called *Gordon presses* in design.

The platen press makes its entire impression in a single moment, so the forces making the impression must be evenly balanced, or one part of the form, usually a corner, will print with too much force. To adjust the press for the different pressures needed for different forms, the gap between the platen and the bed can be widened or narrowed with impression screws, usually provided near the four corners of the platen.

Platen presses may be hand powered, foot powered, or motorized. Large ones use a fly wheel to smooth the mechanical motion. Most of these machines are hand fed, though a few were made with automatic feeders, and feeders were sometimes added.

For a foot-powered or motorized platen press, a throw-off is almost a necessity. When a sheet is misfed, the throw-off can be operated to separate the bed and platen slightly so no impression is made. On a small foot-powered press such as a Golding Pearl, it is possible to stop and reverse the press with the treadle to avoid an impression.

Hand-fed platen presses can print from 600 to 1,000 sheets an hour. A speed control will make the press much more efficient: it will match the speed of the press with the speed at which the stock can be safely fed. With stock that is stiff and easy to handle, speeds of 1,500 sheets per hour can be obtained; with very thin papers, much slower speeds are needed. The speed of a foot-powered press is regulated by the speed with which the treadle is worked. Working a foot treadle for an hour, however, is fairly difficult labor.

Platen presses range in size from miniature to large, with table top presses from 2 × 4 inches to 11 × 16, and floor model presses from 5 × 8 inches to 14 × 22. They range in strength from light to heavy, with the especially heavy ones designed for die cutting or embossing. Their impression and inking is less precise than that of the cylinder press, but they are rapid and are especially suited for business cards, invitations, envelopes, book covers, and small flyers. I often recommend that fine printers who work with proof presses add a platen press to their shop. The tools, type, furniture and supplies that they already use will service both kinds of presses, and platen presses ease much of the drudgery of long runs. For hobby printers, platens are often the press of choice, because they are small, fast, and sufficiently precise.

Accessories can be added to a large platen press, including an ink fountain, an impression counter, and a brake to stop the press. The ink fountain is useful for very long runs or for forms with large amounts of surface area, such as those containing wood type, woodcuts or linoleum blocks. An impression counter is a help when a specified number of finished sheets must be printed, especially when the run is large. A brake, which bears on the flywheel and brings the press to a quick stop, can save time, and is useful when many changes must be made in the form. But none of these accessories is essential, and all of these functions can be accomplished in other ways by the printer. Ink can be periodically supplied by hand, the thigh can be applied to the flywheel to stop the press, and sheets can be counted by hand.

Ralph Green, who studied the subject, concluded that 123 different treadle-driven platen presses were manufactured between 1840 and 1940 in the U.S. In 1888, 36 different presses were in production. Some were sold without names, and some were renamed by printing supply houses. Though more than a hundred manufacturers marketed platen presses, the twentieth century market was dominated by the Chandler and Price company of Cleveland, which began making presses in 1884.

Some printers refer to all platen presses as *clamshells*. Technically, a clamshell is a platen press whose bed is incorporated in the frame; the bed of a clamshell does not rock toward the platen.

The hand press

The hand press is the oldest style of printing press, and was produced until recent times for commercial use in proofing and large-format printing.

I have printed on both iron and wood hand presses, and find that the lack of an inking system is a major disadvantage. The subject of the hand press is covered fully in Richard-Gabriel Rummonds' *Printing on the Iron Handpress,* published by Oak Knoll Press and the British Library.

There were many different manufactures of these presses. One most often sees those made by Hoe in New York, and Schniedewind in Chicago.

13

Recommended Presses

Following is a list of presses found in North America that the author considers "better" presses. I have excluded large machine cylinder presses because they are used by only a small number of letterpress printers.

Challenge Machinery Co.
Grand Haven, Michigan, and Chicago, Illinois

The Challenge Machinery Company began in 1870 as Shniedewend and Lee, a Chicago electrotype company; its papers and master cuts were reportedly saved from the 1871 Chicago fire after being loaded onto a wagon that was pulled into the shallow waters of Lake Michigan. The company began selling printing machinery, foundry type, and printing supplies in 1873, and established a paper cutter factory in 1887.

In 1893, Shniedewend and Lee reorganized as the Challenge Machinery Company. The company moved from Chicago to Grand Haven, Michigan, in 1903. A foundry was established in 1907, reportedly "fulfilling a Lee family ambition to begin with raw material and produce a finished product, all under one roof."

The company claims to have introduced the industry's first paper drill in 1930. The Challenge Machinery Company, now located in Norton Shores, Michigan, is still producing cutters and bindery equipment.

Challenge manufactured platen presses until about 1910, including a 7 × 11, 8 × 12, 9 × 13, 10 × 15, 12 × 18, 13 × 19, a 14 × 22, and 14½ × 22.

The company is best known for its paper cutters and proof presses. It made hand cylinder presses from 1938–1979. Several of its hand cylinder press models were not of very good quality and are rarely found today, including the boxy Style E, the very simple Style 1534 H, and the MP series, which emulates the Vandercook SP presses with their stationary beds. But

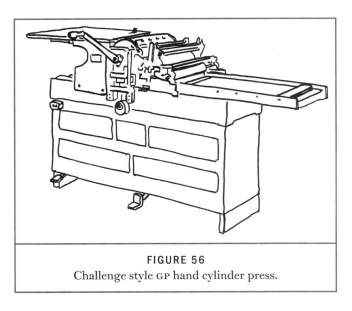

FIGURE 56
Challenge style GP hand cylinder press.

the company's GP and K series are more common and are very useable presses.

The K, KA, KP and GP are really the same press with varying degrees of sophistication. The Style K has no inking system, the KA has a hand-powered ink distribution system, the KP has powered ink distribution, and the GP has powered ink distribution, an automatic gripper release, and an automatic trip for the cylinder, which takes the press off impression while the bed is returned. The three models were made with two bed sizes: 15 × 26 and 20¼ × 26, designated 15 K, 20K, 15KA, 20KA, 15KP, 20KP, 15GP and 20GP. The 15K and 20K weigh 975 and 1,170 pounds, respectively; the 15KA and 20KA weigh 1,040 and 1,215 lbs; the 15KP and 20KP weigh 1,060 and 1,235 lbs; and the 15GP and 20GP weigh 1,160 and 1,235 lbs.

The GP and KP in both sizes were available as a galley press, with a bed made to accommodate type on a galley.

The Challenge proof press with moveable bed has several practical advantages over the Vandercook. The rollers are very simple to adjust and clean, the operator does not need to take a walk every time an impression is made, and the Challenge does not have to be brought to the end of the printing cycle before being returned to its point of beginning, as does the Vandercook. The paper grippers on the Challenge can be opened at any point during the cylinder's revolution, allowing one to remove the sheet when it is most convenient. The Challenge press does require more room, since the bed extends beyond both ends of the press; on both the 15 × 26 and the 20¼ × 26, the bed projects 17 inches from each end of the press when fully extended.

Chandler and Price
Cleveland, Ohio

Usually referred to as "C&P," this company made small, medium, and large platen presses from 1884 to 1964. This was America's most popular manufacturer of platen presses, with an estimated total production of more than 100,000 presses. Fred Williams, who studied its history, claimed that more than 90% of the platen presses in use in the 1930s were C&Ps.

The company began after Harrison T. Chandler, a banker from Chandlerville, Illinois, met William H. Price, the son of a printing press builder, in 1881; they formed a partnership, selling supplies to printers. In 1884 the company introduced two platen presses: the 7 × 11 and the 10 × 15. In 1895, they began selling their own paper cutters. In 1901, they purchased the Gordon factory in Rahway, New Jersey, and the right to use the "Gordon" name. Chandler died in 1912, Price in 1895.

C&P Pilot

The C&P Pilot is a small but strong lever-activated table top press. It has a 6½ × 10″ chase and weighs 195 pounds. It was made with both a stirrup-style and a straight operating lever that could be moved from one side of the press to the other. It was reportedly introduced in 1886, a few years after the Chandler and Price Company was formed. Around 1950, a "new model" Pilot was introduced and the press lost its nineteenth-century styling. It was manufactured until 1962.

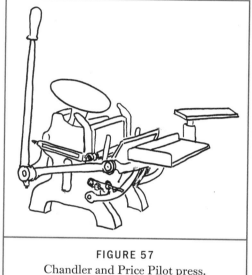

FIGURE 57
Chandler and Price Pilot press.

Curiously, the impression screws on this press are turned *counter-clockwise* to tighten and bring the platen away from the bed. This makes adjustment confusing for those familiar with C&P's larger presses, whose screws are turned *clockwise* to tighten.

The Pilot was used extensively in schools for teaching printing. Many companies produced similar presses, and several writers have noted that the design was not original. In recent times an imported version, the American Pilot, was sold by the American Printing Equipment & Supply Co., in New York. The Craftsmen Machinery Co. of Boston produced a copy of the Pilot called *the Superior,* but its quality was not very good.

Caution is needed when moving this press. If it is lifted by the side arms while in its normal, open position, the press will abruptly close, and on one side, hands will be pinched between the side arm and the small arm that actuates the rollers. This press should always be moved in a closed position, ideally with the lever tied in place.

C&P machine platens

Medium and large C&P's were made in two versions called "old style" and "new series"; presses in the old style have curved spokes on the flywheel,

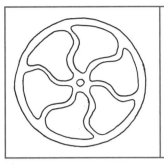 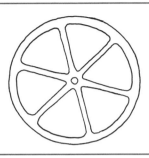

FIGURE 58
Flywheels from an old style (left) and new style (right) Chandler and Price platen press.

while those in the new series have straight spokes. The two versions are generally referred to as "old style" and "new style." The impression screws on old style presses are more difficult to reach and adjust than those on new style presses, but the two versions are quite similar.

C&P machine platens were made in five sizes, including 7 × 11, 8 × 12, 10 × 15, 12 × 18, and 14½ × 22. In the new series, the 7 × 11 was discontinued.

In both the old and new styles, the main shaft was made with a crook to accommodate a treadle.

The old style was manufactured beginning in 1884 and ending, depending on size, from 1911 through 1914. All together, it is estimated that 40,000 old styles were made. The new series models were all introduced in 1911. The 12 × 18 was the first to be discontinued (in 1941); the other sizes were discontinued between 1962 and 1965. A list of dates of manufacture by serial number appears as appendix II.

The most popular sizes were and are 8 × 12, 10 × 15, and 12 × 18. Many 8 × 12's and 10 × 15's survive.

C&P introduced a "Craftsman" line in 1921, marketed for the best quality work, with sizes 10 × 15, 12 × 18, and 14½ × 22. The Craftsman was made with a heavy, one-piece frame, four form rollers, two vibrators, adjustable rails, and a full fountain. They could be purchased with a Rice automatic feeder. The Craftsman has been called "the ultimate in fine platen presses."

C&P made three "heavy duty units"; and a

FIGURE 59
Chandler and Price 8 × 12 new style platen press.

14½ × 22 "Super Heavy Duty"; a side delivery press in hand-fed and automatic models; a no. 1 cylinder (11 × 15) and a no. 2 cylinder (12 × 18). Manufacture of the cylinder presses ceased in 1957.

The serial number on the C&P platen presses is stamped into the upper left corner of the bed.

Chandler and Price New Series (weight in pounds)

8 × 12	1,050
10 × 15	1,500
12 × 18	2,100
14½ × 22	2,700

Craftsman

10 × 15	1,800
10 × 15	2,230 (platen adjusted with hand wheels)
12 × 18	2,500
12 × 18	3,050 (platen adjusted with hand wheels)
14½ × 22	3,075
14½ × 22	3,800 (platen adjusted with hand wheels)

Craftsman Heavy Duty

14½ × 22	3,800
14½ × 22	4,825 with feeder

Colt's Armory style platen press
(Various manufacturers)

This is one of the finest platen presses for inking and impression. It uses a set of rollers as the ink reservoir, some of which oscillate. It also uses the *parallel impression* system invented by Merritt Gally, which rotated the platen directly with a gear train. This press and others emulating it were sold as the Universal, Victoria, National, Hartford and Laureate. All of these presses are heavily built and provide a powerful impression, though they are not as fast as lighter platen presses. They can still be found in commercial shops, where they are used for die cutting and creasing.

The press has a convoluted history. Merritt Gally completed work on this press in 1873, and 850 platen presses were made by two firms that subcontracted the actual manufacture to the Colt's Patent Firearms Manufacturing Co., of Hartford, Connecticut. Gally then contracted directly with Colt's to build the Universal press, and within a decade 2,000 of them were built.

When the patents on the Universal Press expired, Colt's and John Thomson conspired to make the press themselves, excluding Gally. As Colt's owned all the patterns and manufacturing machinery, Gally was unable to obtain even replacement parts for his own presses.

Gally then subcontracted the building of his press to a company in New Jersey, warning printers that he would take legal action against anyone purchasing a press from Colt's.

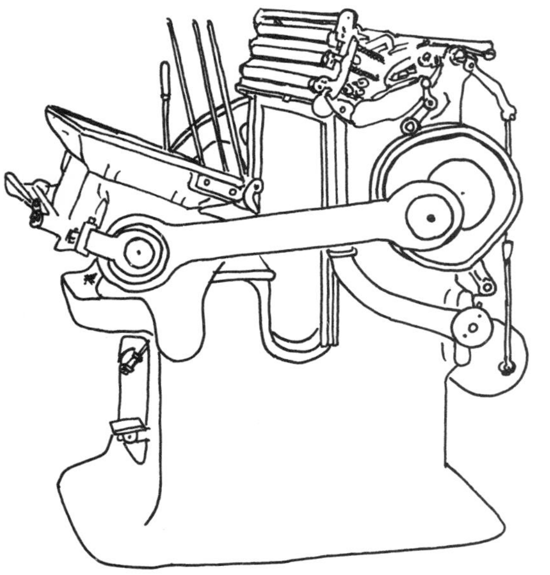

FIGURE 60
Colt's Armory style press made by Thomson.

Gally introduced and patented an "improved" Universal model, made in four sizes: the No. 6, (8 × 12); No. 7, (10 × 15); No. 8, (12 × 18); and No. 21, (15 × 21). The press was sold by The American Type Founders Company.

Thomson began manufacturing a press with most of the features of Gally's Universal Press, calling it the Colt's Armory Universal. A court ruled that Gally's patents had expired, and that the word "Universal" designated a type of press and was not a trademark. In 1902 Thomson acquired the Colt's Press Division and built his own plant at Long Island City, N.Y. He began calling the press "the Colt's Armory press."

In 1910 the National Machine Co., of Hartford, Conn., began to build Gally's Universals. In 1915 Gally sold all his interest in the press to National, which continued to build both the old and improved versions as the Hartford and National.

The Thomson Co. continued to make the Colt's Armory in four sizes: 8 × 12, 10 × 15, 13 × 19 and 14 × 22. In 1923 the John Thomson Co. and the National Machine Company merged to become the Thomson-National Press Co. The next year the firm purchased the factory of Golding and Co. at Franklin, Massachusetts, which had previously been acquired by the American Type Founders Company.

It is unclear when manufacture of the press ceased. Hoch, writing in 1943, shows a 10 × 15 "Thomson-National Quarto Medium" (weighing 1,673 pounds), a 13 × 19 "Thomson-National Half Medium," (weighing 2,625 pounds), a 14 × 22 Colt's Armory (weighing 3,030 pounds), and a 14 × 22 Laureate (weighing 3,585 pounds). The presses are all hand-fed.

Golding and Company
Boston, Massachusetts

Golding and Company made many presses, but its best-known is the Pearl, a floor-model platen press made in several sizes. The smallest Pearls are the most common and most desired today. Golding's other presses included the Peerless, the Official (including the well-known *map press,* with a stationary platen and a moving bed), the Golding Jobber, the Art Jobber, and the Fairhaven newspaper cylinder. The firm sold type and equipment as well. For a short time after William Golding's death in 1916, his two sons continued the business, but sold to the American Type Founders Company in 1918. The factory in Franklin, Massachusetts, was sold to the Thomson-National Press Co., and in 1927, production ended.

Official

The Official was probably introduced in 1871; by 1881 it was available in several sizes, from 2 × 3 inches to 10 × 15, designated the Junior, 1, 2, 3, 4, 6, 7, 9, and 12. Their weight (in pounds), as shown below, includes their shipping boxes:

Junior	2 × 3	
1	3 × 4 ½	
2	4 × 6	60
3	5 × 7 ½	93
4	6 × 9	120
6	8¼ × 12½	260
7	10 × 15	
9	6 × 9	
12	8¼ × 12½	

All of the Officials lacked side arms and could accommodate very large sheets.

Models 9 and 12 were made with a moving platen and a stationary bed, making them particularly suited to printing in the margins of architectural drawings and maps. These came to be known as the *map press.*

Pearl

The Pearl is sought after by those looking for a compact machine press. Introduced in 1869 by William Golding, it was first made in two sizes: the Number 1 (5 × 8 inches); and the Number 3 (7 × 11 inches). The Pearl had a stationary bed, but no throw-off or grippers. The Number 1, 3, and 5 are referred to as *old style,* with no throw-off and two rollers.

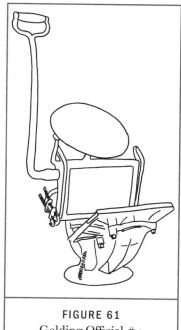

FIGURE 61
Golding Official #4 platen press.

The "improved Pearl" was introduced in 1895. It was heavier than the original model and was equipped with a throw-off and three rollers, rather than two. In the improved model, the ink disk can be set to revolve clockwise or counter clock-wise.

The old style models continued to be assembled, however, after 1895.

The early models were packed in a wood box that became the base. Later models had a base of cast iron.

The serial number of a Pearl is located at the center of the top of the bed, below the ink disk. But this number reflects only the sequence of presses built in that year. For a time, Golding cast the year of manufacture into the side of the base.

In 1936 the Craftsmen Machinery Company of Dedham, Massachusetts, acquired patterns for the 7×11 Improved Pearl and offered the press as the CMC jobber until about 1955. The company reportedly still has the materials to manufacture the press.

Six models of the Pearl were made; their weight (in pounds), as shown below, includes their shipping boxes:

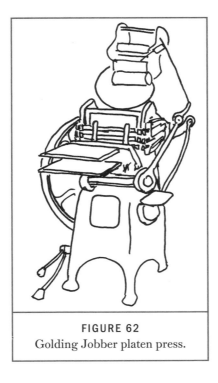

FIGURE 62
Golding Jobber platen press.

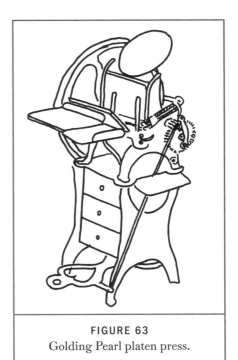

FIGURE 63
Golding Pearl platen press.

Model 1	5 × 8	400
Model 3	7 × 11	
Model 5	9 × 14	1,100
Model 8	5 × 8	500
Model 11	7 × 11	730
Model 14	9 × 14	1,100

Peerless

The Peerless has a "gooseneck" arm which drives the platen; because the gooseneck is attached to the platen's center, the impression is easily balanced. The press incorporates a counterweight to smooth its action. It was said to be a favorite for creasing and cutting cardboard boxes.

Jobber and Art Jobber

The Golding Jobber and Art Jobber are sturdy and include sophisticated inking systems. In addition to a conventional ink disk, some models have an ink distributor beneath the bed which gives a new layer of ink to the rollers before they return over the type on their upward movement. The Jobber (with three rollers) was made in 8 × 12, 10 × 15, 12 × 18 and 15 × 21 sizes. The Art Jobber (with four rollers) was made in 12 × 18 and 15 × 21 sizes; the latter weighs 3,250 pounds.

Heidelberg

Schnellpressenfabrik A. Hamm Act.-Ges. (1899);
Schnellpressenfabrik Aktiengesellschaft Heidelberg (1905).

Heidelberg, Germany

Heidelberg was one of the few foreign manufacturers to successfully market letterpress presses in the U.S. A well-known maker of printing equipment, the Heidelberg company introduced its legendary *Tiegel* or platen press in 1914. Because of the rotating motion of the feeding arms, the press came to be known as the *Windmill* in the U.S.

Heidelberg claims that, in 1926, it became the first German printing press maker to use assembly-line production, and at that time 100 Windmills were shipped from the factory each month. The company mounted working Windmills in buses which were driven to print shops where the machines were demonstrated while printing. The company also financed the presses, and promoted the motto: "the Heidelberger pays for itself." By 1967, the company had built 175,000 of the presses.

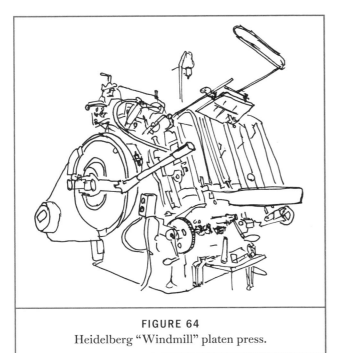

FIGURE 64
Heidelberg "Windmill" platen press.

The Windmill is a sophisticated platen press with a high speed and the ability to handle many different weights of paper stock. It has a fixed bed and a unique knee and lever link to actuate the platen. It uses an automatic pressure oiling system, and is equipped with a large, cylindrical ink reservoir. Automatically fed, it can print with the paper held against guides located below the tympan, or with the paper held by the arms of the windmill-like feeder. It features precise register, and easy adjustments for register, impression, and roller height. Makeready can be done very quickly. It carries two form rollers; an air blast from one side of the bed helps to separate the sheet and the form.

The Windmill was made in two sizes, 10 × 15 inches (models T and TP) and 13 × 18, (models GT, GTK, GTP and GTS) capable of producing 5,000 and 4,000 impressions per hour, respectively. The GTK was designed for printing, cutting, and creasing, the model GTP for printing and foil stamping, and the model GTS for cutting and creasing.

The Windmill has a reputation for dependability and is sought by commercial printers still using letterpress processes. One sometimes hears stories of press operators who would leave the press running while they left the premises to eat lunch.

The press is provided with 1¾" holes in the base, into which steel rods can be inserted for lifting points. A lifting eye can also be bolted to the press though a hole under the chase clip. The chase clip and a sheetmetal cover must both be removed; on the back of the press, a door gives access.

Kelly Automatic

American Type Founders Company
Jersey City, New Jersey

William M. Kelly, a salesman for American Type Founders, developed a small automatic cylinder press with L.B. Barber and H.H. Edge in 1911. Robert Nelson, president of ATF, took an interest, and the Model B was introduced in 1914. The bed was just over 19 × 22, and the press, which could run at 3,600 impressions per hour, could handle a 14 × 22 inch sheet. Model A was introduced at an unknown date; it weighs 4,270 pounds, or

4,700 with extended delivery. Model C was introduced in 1937 with an automatic lubrication system and other improvements.

In 1922, a heavier model, the Number 2, was introduced; it could handle a 22 × 34 inch sheet and weighed 10,350 pounds. The Number 1, introduced at an unknown date, could handle a sheet 22 × 28, and weighed 9,235 pounds. In 1949 the Number 3 was introduced that could handle a 25 × 37 inch sheet.

When Kelly retired in 1949, 11,000 Kelly presses had been sold, but the popularity of the line soon declined, and the last press was made in the U.S. in 1954. The British company Vickers continued manufacturing the Kelly c and Number 3 until 1957.

Another, little-known press, the Kelly Automatic Jobber, could run at 4,500 impressions per hour, and could handle a

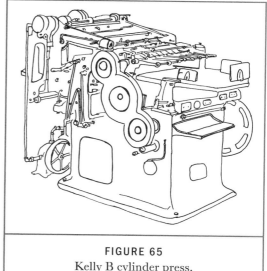

FIGURE 65
Kelly B cylinder press.

13 × 19½ inch sheet. The Jobber, introduced in 1925, incorporated an inclined bed and weighed 4,000 pounds, 4,500 with extended delivery. It was manufactured for only a few years.

Kelsey Press Co.
Meriden, Connecticut

Established in 1872, Kelsey produced light but well-designed small and medium sized platen presses. The company once manufactured treadle-powered platen presses, but Kelsey is known today for its table-top platens. It marketed its presses largely as outfits for hobby printers, businesses, and institutions that wanted to do their own printing. Ink, type, cabinets, tools and paper stock could be purchased from the company.

Kelsey's table top presses included the Excelsior and the Victor.

The Excelsior, powered by hand with a front lever, was made in many sizes: 3 × 5, 5 × 8, 6 × 10, 9 × 13, and 11 × 16 inches. Their weights boxed were 45, 100, 150, 350, and 550 pounds, respectively. All have a removable bed which doubles as an imposing surface for preparing the form.

To secure the form in the chase, these presses use screws extending through the sides of the chase, rather than quoins. The Excelsior is the Kelsey model which one usually sees today.

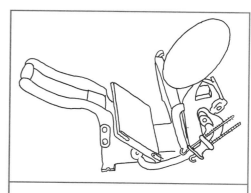

FIGURE 66
Kelsey Excelsior platen press.

The Excelsior is an excellent choice for someone needing the most portable, or the smallest, of presses. It is a good choice for the printer who wants to work in a limited space or store the press when not in use. It requires only simple tools to operate: a slotted screwdriver and a small wrench will suffice. The operating lever serves as a carrying handle, making the press easy to move. The ink disk is removable, however, and may fall away unless the press is allowed to hang by the operating lever.

The platen is rather slightly built. On the smallest size, it measures 5½ × 3¾ inches but is only ¼ of an inch thick. The press can be temperamental to operate. The printer must particularly watch that the clamp, which holds both the platen and chase, is properly seated each time it is used. If it is not, the bed will not be held in the correct position in relation to the platen.

The Victor, which resembles the Pilot press of Chandler and Price, is powered by hand and carries a 6 × 9 chase. It weighs 150 pounds, boxed. The side hand lever can be dismounted and moved from one side of the press to the other.

Kelsey's Star is a treadle-powered press. The Star was first manufactured by George Prouty; it is 7 × 11 inches and weighs 500 pounds with shipping box.

Finally, Kelsey made two platen presses that were designed to be run by treadle or belt. The King is 9 × 13, and was designed by George Prouty, apparently for Kelsey. The Union is 10 × 14 and weighs 850 pounds boxed.

In 1990, Kelsey announced that it would sell its existing inventory and not manufacture any more presses. It claimed that it sold 1,850 presses in 1958, but fewer than 100 presses in the years prior to 1990, and sales had declined from $1 million in 1981 to less than $200,000 five years later.

Kluge

Brandtjen and Kluge Co.
St. Paul, Minnesota

The Brandtjen and Kluge Co. began manufacturing vacuum-powered feeders for presses in 1919. In 1931 the company began selling the feeder attached to their own platen presses: a 10 × 15 Model M press and a 12 × 18 Model N press. The presses were popular, and by World War II, Brandtjen and Kluge were shipping 300 presses per month.

The company is now based in St. Croix Falls, Wisconsin, and continues to sell foil stamping and embossing equipment. A few offset presses are also made. A large foil stamping and embossing press, the VS 2028, has 200 tons of impression strength and handles sheet sizes to 24 × 30″.

Kluge Automatic

This automatic platen press was and is widely used for die cutting, embossing, and foil work, and is capable of feeding a variety of stock, from "onion skin to wallboard." Early models borrowed heavily from the C&P platen press.

The 10 × 15 will print a sheet 12 × 16 inches, and weighs 2,500 lbs. The 12 × 18 will print a sheet 14 × 19 inches, and weighs 3,450 lbs. Both have four form rollers and an ink distributing roller atop each pair of form rollers. A few parts on the press are made of aluminum, in order to keep both the center of gravity and the weight of the moving parts low.

In 1946, the MA and NA models were introduced, which were replaced by the MB and NB models two years later. In 1959, the company introduced the Model C with sealed ball bearings, and then, at an unknown date, the 11 × 17 and 13 × 19 D Series. The press continues in production today, as the 13 × 19 HD, (introduced in 1963), and the 14 × 22 EHD (introduced in 1967), a press whose impression can be adjusted while the press is running. Company president Hank Brandtjen told the author in 2005 that the firm sells about one press with ink equipment each year, making this, it appears, the last letterpress printing press in production. The presses sell for about $60,000.

The 11 × 17 ought to be called a 10 × 15, which is the size of its chase, but the company marketed it as an 11 × 17, the size of the largest sheet that could be fed. It is capable of 4,000 impressions per hour, and weighs 2,250 pounds.

While it is possible to swing the feeder away from the press and feed a Kluge Automatic by hand, it is very difficult because of the short dwell time and a lack of space. The company also sold hand-fed presses in 10 × 15 and 12 × 18 inch sizes which weighed 1,900 and 2,785 pounds, respectively. The hand-fed presses are rare.

The company now officially warns against the hand feeding of any of its presses.

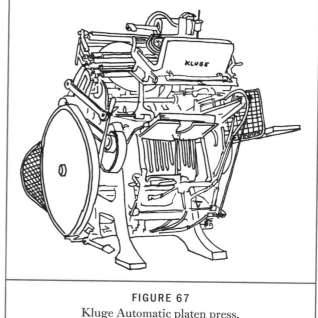

FIGURE 67
Kluge Automatic platen press.

Miehle
Miehle Printing Press & Manufacturing Co.
Chicago

Miehle Vertical

Chicago printer Robert Miehle founded the Miehle Printing Press & Manufacturing Co. to build a flat-bed cylinder press in about 1890. The company came to dominate the flatbed cylinder press market, making presses ranging from the Pony (21 × 30½ in the chase) to the Number 7-0 (45 × 70 in the chase).

FIGURE 68
Miehle Vertical cylinder press.

In 1921, Miehle acquired the design of Edward Chesire for a small cylinder press with a two-revolution cylinder and a bed mounted vertically. To limit the size of the press and increase its speed, both the bed and the cylinder moved. After a few design changes, production of the Miehle Vertical began in the same year with the v-36. The "v" designated "vertical," and the number indicated the number of impressions, in hundreds, that the press could produce per hour. In 1931, the v-45 model was introduced, with a maximum form size of 12¼ × 19.

The v-50 model was introduced in 1940, with a change in styling and an automatic lubrication system. The maximum sheet size was increased to 14 × 20 inches. Production was curtailed during World War II, and was resumed with a number of new features, including a third form roller and a throw-off.

In an era when other manufacturers were discontinuing their small cylinder presses, Miehle continued to produce its verticals. The v-50x, enclosed in a box of sheet metal, made its debut in 1964. The last Vertical was built in July, 1978.

The Miehle v-36 weighs about 2,550 pounds, the v-45 weighs about 2,800 pounds.

Sigwalt Manufacturing Co.
Chicago

This is a lesser-known, but well-loved line of presses. Despite their slight appearance, Sigwalt users report excellent impressional strength. The presses are said to be well-balanced, and commercial printers reportedly used them for very small jobs. The absence of side arms on the press meant they could handle very large sheets, such as maps and signs.

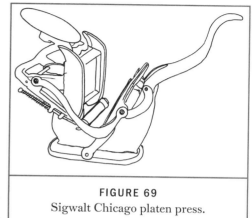

FIGURE 69
Sigwalt Chicago platen press.

John Sigwalt immigrated from France to Illinois, where he apprenticed as a machinist. He manufactured sewing machines until the Chicago fire of 1871, then made stamping equipment. The Sigwalt Company was incorporated by 1883.

Sigwalt introduced two small presses in the late nineteenth century. The *Chicago* has a front operating lever and was sold either with or without an inking system. It was made in two sizes, the largest being 2¼ × 4 inches — not large enough to be considered more than a toy press.

The *Nonpareil* has a side lever and was made in five sizes, ranging from 2½ × 4 to 6 × 9. The press was sold by the Acme Type Foundry and others, including Sears Roebuck and Company. The Nonpareil was apparently remodeled as the *Ideal*, which was made in four of the Nonpareil's sizes.

The Sigwalt Company is not credited with much originality. Elizabeth Harris called the company's Chicago press "a copy of Dorman's Baltimorean." Fred Williams wrote that Sigwalt's 4 × 6 Nonpareil and their 5 × 7½ Ideal were based on Golding's Officials of the same size.

Nonpareil number 21	2½ × 4″
Nonpareil number 22	3 × 4½″
Nonpareil number 23	4 × 6″
Nonpareil number 24	5 × 7½″ (stirrup handle)
Nonpareil number 25	6 × 9″ (stirrup handle)
Ideal number 2	3 × 5″
Ideal number 3	4 × 6″, weight 60 lbs
Ideal number 4	5 × 7½″, weight 90 lbs
Ideal number 5	6 × 9″ weight 125 lbs

The Sigwalt Company also sold foundry type and paper. It was acquired by the Bankers and Merchants Rubber Stamp Co. in 1962, and the Sigwalt parts and manufacturing rights were then sold to the Al Frank Printing

Equipment and Supply Co. of Chicago, and then to Elmer Porter in about 1974. Porter, operating the J.E.T. Manufacturing Co., reportedly assembled only a few presses. In 1979, Fred Williams reported that the manufacturing jigs and patterns had been acquired by the Tampico Press in Chicago. Larry Raid of Denmark, Iowa, owns the patterns at this writing.

Vandercook and Sons
Chicago

The Vandercook is widely considered to be the most solid and the best of the proof presses, and its price today reflects that. Most common are the SP, the 219, and the Number 4. The SP15 is the most sought after.

Chicago newspaperman Robert Vandercook founded the Vandercook Co. in 1909 with a "rocker" proof press that used a partial cylinder to make impressions of small forms. A more conventional galley press was introduced in 1911, and a press with a moving carriage in 1914. In 1918 Vandercook's three sons joined him, and the firm became Vandercook and Sons.

In 1925 Vandercook and Sons introduced the Model 3, a hand-powered press with powered ink distribution, designed for proofing photo-engraved plates. This press was the basis for many of the company's subsequent presses.

The company produced sixty different models, and made 30,000 total presses. In 1962 a trade association poll discovered that 81% of all typographic shops in the U.S. were using Vandercook equipment. In 2004, Harold Sterne estimated that 1,000 Vandercook presses were in use.

In 1968, one of Vandercook's suppliers, Illinois Tool Works, purchased the company, and the name "Vandercook and Sons" was discontinued. Four years later, an Illinois Tool Works manager, Hugh Fletcher, purchased the company and renamed it "Vandersons." Vandersons stopped manufacturing presses in 1976, at which point they were producing only four models: HS27, SP20, SP25, and Universal I. The company continued to supply parts and supplies. In 1989 the company was sold to Stuart Evans; in 1993 Harold Sterne and Tom Bell purchased all the equipment and parts from Vander-

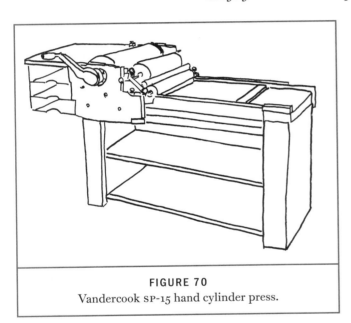

FIGURE 70
Vandercook SP-15 hand cylinder press.

sons Corp. and combined it with their letterpress supply business, NA Graphics, in Cincinnati. In 1996 Fritz Klinke purchased NA Graphics and moved it to Silverton Colorado.

NA Graphics has some parts and supplies available, and many of Vandercook's original drawings. If necessary, they can use the drawings to commission new parts. They also offer to consult their records and tell press owners the date on which their press was shipped from the factory, and the name of the original owner.

Vandercook made other equipment besides presses, and they made proof presses for offset lithography.

The following lists only those presses with both inking systems and paper grippers, thus excluding Vandercook's "composing room cylinder press," and presses 0, 1, 2, and 14. The sizes are taken from Vandercook literature, though some of the measurements for length of bed seem exaggerated.

Model	Size	Weight	Notes
05	15 × 26	800 lbs.	Introduced 1949
15	15 × 26	1,000 lbs.	Powered inking, introduced 1914
SP15	15 × 31½	705 lbs.	Introduced 1961
SP20	20 × 34½	1,440 lbs.	Introduced 1960
SP25	25 × 40½	1,600 lbs.	Introduced 1963
			(hand powered and motor powered models made)
Universal I	15½ × 39	1,300 lbs.	Introduced 1958
Universal II	unknown	unknown	55 made 1958–60 only
Universal III	19 × 42½	1,800 lbs.	Introduced 1959
Number 3	15 × 35	1,000 lbs.	Introduced 1925
Number 4	15 × 35	1,100 lbs.	Made from 1935 to 1960
Number 425	25 × 45	4,200 lbs.	Introduced 1958
Number 219	19 × 41	2,300 lbs.	Introduced 1927
			(hand powered and motor powered models made)
Number 223	23½ × 50	3,900 lbs.	Introduced 1937
Number 226	28 × 45	4,850 lbs.	
Number 320G	20 × 46½	1,850 lbs.	Introduced 1929
Number 325A	25 × 46½	2,000 lbs.	Adjustable bed
			(hand powered and motor powered models made)

The designation "SP" is said to stand for "simple precision." Several models, including the Universal and the 219, were available with an adjustable bed, which the company designated as AB.

On some Vandercook presses, the name of the company inspector appears below the serial number at the end of the press bed; examples are: H.L. Keller, J.H. Lavin, A.W. Winard, and C.G. Zurick. Gene Wenderski, a former company employee, reportedly said that the name "H.L. Keller" was a jest, meant to suggest that Helen Keller had inspected the press.

The serial number on a press can be used to determine the year of manufacture. A list of dates by serial numbers appears as an appendix.

14

Ink & Rollers

Selection of ink

Most letterpress printers use ink designed for offset lithography, either rubber or oil based, which works perfectly well with letterpress processes.

Inks made specifically for letterpress are available, and a manufacturer will mix a pound at a time for you. Letterpress ink typically has less tack and less pigment than lithographic ink, because letterpress printing typically deposits more ink than lithographic printing.

A few letterpress printers prefer lithographic ink made for stone lithography, or undiluted etching ink made for intaglio printing. These inks, available from art supply houses, give a rich, flat appearance. Avoid inks formulated for linoleum or woodcut, or those called *relief inks*. These are usually too soupy. When ink is the proper consistency for letterpress printing, a gob of it will not "flow."

For a hundred years, ink makers have entreated printers not to supplement their inks with additives, and I have generally heeded that advice. The exception is my use of burnt plate oil, used routinely by intaglio printers to dilute their inks. I use this only when I find an ink that is too heavy, and won't roll out on the press well; I add the oil in minute quantities.

Use of ink

When inking a press, be careful to apply too little, rather than too much, ink. If a press is over-inked, the proof will be sloppy-looking, with the edges of the type poorly defined. When this occurs, some of the ink must be removed from the press. I usually do this with solvent, which must be taken up, as much as possible, with clean rags. It is much easier to clean ink from a metal surface than the soft surface of a roller. Cleaning the ink disk of a platen press, or the steel drum or distributor roller of a cylinder press, is usually sufficient to reduce the amount of ink on an over-inked press; you don't need to clean the entire inking system. Some printers prefer to use paper to absorb some of the ink; they place a sheet on the ink disk of a platen press, and then roll the ink rollers over the sheet; on a cylinder press, they feed a sheet between two ink rollers. Some papers will leave a lot of lint in the remaining ink, so if you adopt this method, use an appropriate paper.

Surfaces with large solid areas like linoleum cuts, photoengravings, wood type, or wood engravings require much more ink than does small type, and it's usually necessary to print such things in a separate press run.

Ink seems to creep a bit as it sets; printing will often appear more heavily inked the next day, when the ink is dry, than at press side. It is always preferable to err on the side of too little ink.

When books are printed, careful attention must be paid to the consistency of the inking between the front and back of the sheet, and between gatherings. Type which is more heavily inked will appear bolder and have more contrast, and the discrepancy will be obvious.

Drier

Drier is often added by the manufacturer to make ink dry more quickly on the printed sheet. The amount added will determine how long you can leave the ink on a press before it solidifies. Some ink will dry overnight, while other ink will remain workable for days or weeks.

Drier can also be added by the printer. Japan drier, sold for oil paint, works well with printing ink. Drier is especially useful when large areas or *solids* are being printed, from woodcuts or wood type, for example. Without drier, solids will require many days to dry.

Handling ink

When working with ink, have at hand some waste paper and an ink knife. A clean glass, metal, or stone surface can be used to mix colors and roll out ink. Open the ink can and scrape off any dried ink from the ink surface, discarding it on a sheet of waste paper. If a can is new, I discard the paper cover which is found beneath the metal cover, but many printers re-use it. Remove ink from the can with shallow strokes of the knife; this prevents the ink from developing pits, which speeds its drying. Keep the ink can covered, except when extracting ink.

A shop should have several ink knives available for mixing colors. Paint knives from a hardware store serve well. Slugs can be substituted for ink knives when necessary. If ink cans are difficult to open, try heating their tops gently on a stove, with a hair drier, or by torch.

Most printers clean the ink off of their press at the end of each day. But I often leave ink sitting on a press overnight if I know I will be printing again the next day. I sometimes leave ink for several days, but I check it daily to determine if it is beginning to set.

Transparent ink

Transparent ink is used when a pastel effect is wanted, or when one ink is printed over another. The transparent ink can be mixed with a small amount of regular ink for coloring. Magnesium carbonate and plate oil can be mixed with ink to make it more transparent.

Color

Ink colors are described by the PMS or Pantone Matching System, which is universally used in the printing industry. A book of color swatches is sold by Pantone, and the *PMS number* from the book can be used to order ink from a manufacturer. The PMS swatch books show formulas for mixing all of the PMS colors using a few basic inks. But one can also mix most, though not all, colors by eye, using the three primary colors: blue, yellow, and red. It is best to mix the darker color into the lighter one. A few colors require a base color brighter than the primary. If a color must be mixed repeatedly and exactness is required, the constituent inks can be measured by weight.

Theoretically, metallic inks can be mixed by adding metal powders to inks, but most printers order metallic colors already mixed from a manufacturer.

In commercial full-color printing, variants of the three primaries and black are used: cyan, magenta, and yellow, often abbreviated as "CMYK." The terms *four-color* and *process color* are used to describe full color printing.

Artists have their own vocabulary for describing colors. *Hue* refers to what, in common parlance, is called *color*. A *tint* is a color mixed with white, a *tone* is a color mixed with gray, and a *shade* is a color mixed with black. *Warm colors* are reds, oranges, and yellows, while *cool colors* are greens, blues, and violets.

A color wheel, available from art supply stores, is a useful tool for the letterpress shop. When mixing or testing an ink color, smear the thinnest layer possible on the stock that is to be used. There is often substantial difference in the hue of an ink when seen in bulk and when seen in a thin film.

Color *names* are trouble: it is unreliable to specify colors by name. When working with someone from a distance, it's best to send them to their local print shop to consult a Pantone book.

Any color can be carried on a printing press. When inking a press with a light color you may need to clean the press, apply the color, and clean the press a second time to remove all traces of previous ink colors.

It is possible to print with two colors at once on any press if the distributing system, which moves ink across the rollers, is disabled. The *split fountain* is formed when one color is placed on one side of the rollers, and a second color on the other. When the distribution roller is removed or held out of the way (on a cylinder press) or the ink disk is made stationary (on a platen press), the two colors will remain on their respective sides of the rollers. Without the distribution system, however, the ink won't be carried evenly across its share of the roller surface until the rollers have turned for a rather long time. If the two colors are to appear within the same area on the printed form, the work and turn method, described on page 150, can be used.

Hand rolling

When applying ink to type by hand, use substantially less ink than you would carry on a machine-mounted roller. Use a soft roller, avoiding the hard rollers made for inking linoleum or woodcut.

It's difficult to apply ink evenly by hand. When hand inking, apply the ink to a corner of the ink-rolling surface, roll out thoroughly in a small area, and then lift the brayer and move it to a clean area of the rolling surface. This is an easy way to control the amount of ink you roll onto the type.

Roller bearers, wide strips of type-high material, help to keep the ink roller from slurring and from wiping the type clean, rather than inking it. The roller bearers are placed beside the type block, but far enough away so that they print outside the sheet.

Automatic inking

Most presses are equipped with an automatic system for rolling ink onto the type. On a cylinder press, the system typically includes a plate or cylinder which serves as a reservoir to supply the system; distribution rollers to move the ink from the reservoir to the form rollers and make it even across the press; and two or more form rollers, which lay the ink on the form. On a platen press, the system typically consists of a disk for a reservoir and a series of form rollers; a few platen presses also use distribution rollers.

Rollers are carried to the form while revolving at a controlled speed: they must roll over the type without wiping the ink from it. On cylinder presses, the roller speed is determined by a gear system which engages a gear track on one or both sides of the bed. On a platen press, roller speed is determined by wheels or *trucks* which are fixed to the roller shafts and ride on a bearing rail on each side of the bed.

Because the roller is soft, it can accommodate some discrepancy between its actual and ideal speed: that is, between the speed given to it by the trucks or gears, and the speed it would have if it were free to roll directly over the type. If the difference is very great, either turning too fast or too slow, the roller surface will wipe the ink from the form as it passes. But the difference in speeds is usually small enough so the roller surface will deliver a uniform layer of ink by distorting slightly while passing over the form.

Cylinder presses are fitted with slow-moving form rollers of large diameter that are rather forgiving of differences in actual and ideal roller speed. On cylinder presses, roller speed isn't usually problematic and roller speeds are usually not adjustable. Platen presses, however, are fitted with small form rollers that spin rather rapidly, and a match in speeds is more

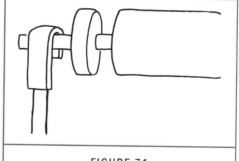

FIGURE 71
Platen press saddle, truck, and roller
(left to right).

important. Many platen presses are fitted with adjustable roller trucks, which control roller speed as well as the height of the rollers above the form. A few platen presses (Kluge, Heidelberg, and the C&P Craftsman series) have adjustable roller tracks, which move away from and toward the bed to adjust the roller height.

The height of the rollers above the form is an important adjustment that is used to control the amount of ink that is transferred to the type with each pass of the rollers. Rollers, particularly those made of composition, change their diameter with changes in temperature and humidity, and the roller height must be constantly adjusted, albeit slightly. This adjustment is done differently on cylinder presses and platen presses, and they are discussed separately below.

Note that some presses are made with bearers that are not type high, and the bearers, even if made type high, may be worn. This may affect the proper setting of the form rollers on that press.

Whenever ink is suspected as a source of trouble in printing, the printer should observe the image left on the surface of the roller after the form removes some of the ink. If the image is slurred, there is a problem with roller height and/or speed. It is also helpful to inspect the form: sometimes one can see variations in the amount of ink on the face of the type, or one can see that ink is being rolled onto the non-printing parts of the type, leads, or furniture.

On any press, roller bearers can be used within the form; these are discussed in the section on hand inking above. I can recall using them only once or twice, when no amount of adjustment on an errant press would correct an inking problem. Other printers use them regularly.

Roller setting gauge

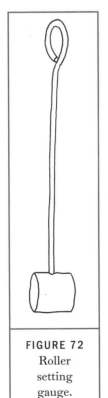

FIGURE 72
Roller
setting
gauge.

The height of each form roller should be consistent from side to side, and the height of each form roller should match the others on the press.

A roller setting gauge is useful for adjusting form roller heights quickly and consistently on either a platen or a cylinder press. The gauge is a narrow, type-high cylinder which can be turned onto its side, slid along the press bed, and righted near the relevant roller. While the gauge is held in place on the bed, the roller is moved over it, leaving a line of ink on the surface of the gauge. The line of ink varies in width according to the height of the roller, and the widths can be compared for each roller, and for each side of the roller. If the roller gauge is turned upside down after being marked, two lines of ink can be left on its surface, and the two lines can be easily compared.

With synthetic rollers, the line of ink left on the gauge should be about $\frac{1}{16}$ of an inch in width. With composition rollers, the line should be about $\frac{1}{8}$ of an inch.

The gauge may reveal a deposit of ink that is light: that is, the *width* of the streak made on each side of the roller is consistent, but one side of the roller leaves a thinner film of ink—there is an obvious difference in *color*. This usually indicates that the distribution rollers are not making proper contact with the form rollers, and are not distributing the ink across the width of the press.

A roller setting gauge may easily be made by a machinist. Two important features are a narrow width, so the gauge can be laid on its side and slid beneath a roller without being marked, and a handle with some bulk and flatness, for easy toppling.

Cylinder press

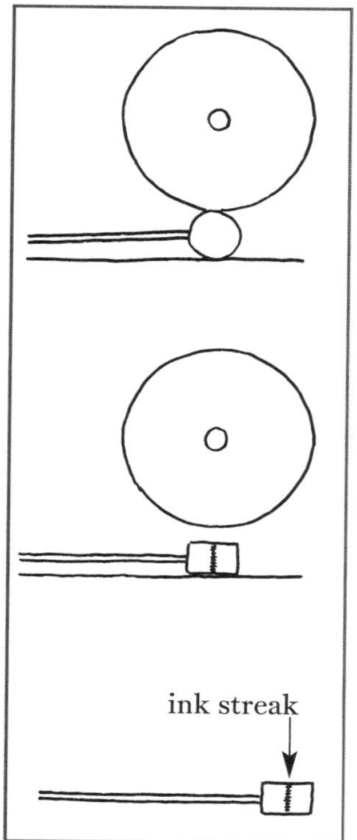

On a cylinder press, roller height is adjusted with screws that raise and lower the roller cradles. On many presses, the adjusting screws are accompanied by set screws that can be used either to lock the adjusting screws in place, or provide enough friction to prevent their turning from the vibration of the press. On some presses, a change in roller height affects the amount of contact between the form rollers and the distribution rollers, and the two must be adjusted together.

One should periodically examine the inking system on a cylinder press to ensure the proper working of the clutch which disengages the form rollers from the motor and engages the roller driving gear against the gear track on the bed. When these clutches fail, contact with the form will still turn the rollers, making the defect difficult to notice.

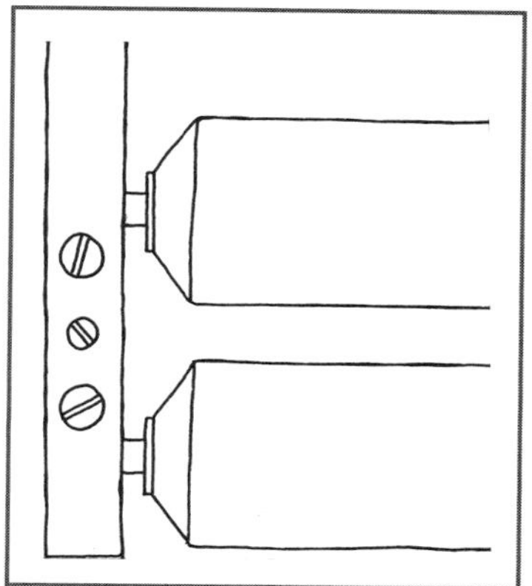

Platen press

On a platen press, roller heights are set after observing the image made by the type on the roller surface, by sighting down the length of the roller for consistency, or by using a roller setting gauge, described above.

Roller height is adjusted in one of three ways. The most primitive involves building up the surface of the bearing rails at each side of the bed. Occasionally, the press comes supplied with a series of roller trucks of different diameters that can be fitted on the roller shaft. On larger presses, the adjustment is made by altering the diameter of the roller trucks, which are adjustable or *expandable*. The last two methods are ideal, because they alter both the height of the roller and the roller speed.

With fixed roller trucks, the adjustment is made only

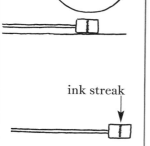

FIGURE 73
A roller setting gauge is laid on the bed and inked (top). When being placed on or retracted from the press, the gauge can be laid on its side to clear an adjacent roller (center). The streak of ink left on the surface of the gauge is used in adjusting roller height (bottom).

FIGURE 74
Form roller height adjusting screws on a Vandercook 219. The center screw is a set screw.

when the diameter of the roller is noticeably larger than the diameter of the truck. Tape or cardboard is applied to the bearing rail to lift the rollers away from the form.

With adjustable roller trucks, I make the trucks the same diameter as the rollers by sighting down the length of the rollers. Other printers set the trucks slightly smaller than the roller diameter.

Kinds of rollers

Roller materials include urethane, rubber (also called nitrile or butyl nitrate), pvc, and composition. Urethane and rubber are tough, but have mediocre ink characteristics. pvc, said to resist the mechanical shock of letterpress, has great ink holding.

A more traditional roller material is composition, made of hide glue, molasses, and glycerin. Composition rollers contract and swell with changes in temperature and humidity, may be attractive to rodents, and are quickly damaged if exposed to water or excessive heat. However, they are preferred by many for their superior inking qualities. pvc, however, is said to be comparable to composition in inking quality.

Cleaning ink from the press

Ink is cleaned with solvent which is either poured onto a rag or directly onto the ink rollers and disk or drum. I usually pour the solvent directly on the rollers and press. On my cylinder presses I place a clean rag beneath the rollers to avoid soiling the bed. On some presses, such as the Vandercook 219, the form rollers are designed to be lifted off the press as a unit to make cleaning easier.

When cleaning rollers, clean the sides as well, so ink doesn't build up there. The choice of solvent is important, and should be matched with the roller material. A commercial printing supply house can provide advice; several washes are now available that are both kinder to the roller material and less toxic for the printer. Mineral spirits and white gas are considered by some to be hard on rollers, and some printers have turned to such things as vegetable shortening.

Care of rollers

Rollers can be stored in place on the press after cleaning, but they should be left so that the surface has no contact with other rollers, the form, or the ink disk. Most printers leave expandable roller trucks on a platen press; while not ideal, prolonged rest against the bearing rails does not seem to shorten their life. The spring pressure exerted against the trucks can be reduced by leaving the rollers positioned over the center of the bed.

If rollers are stored off the press, the shafts should be supported in a rack or by blocks or other supports so that the roller surface has no contact with anything. Furniture makes a convenient temporary support.

Rollers should be protected from dirt, moisture, high temperatures and direct sunlight. Eventually, a glaze of ink forms on the surface and lowers the ability of the roller to hold ink. A deglazing solvent is available to remedy this. With time, rollers become pitted and scored, and must be replaced. Some printers keep a set of rollers that are in poor condition for forms which are likely to damage rollers, such as forms with perforating rule.

A roller with a cut or damaged surface can be temporarily repaired with vinyl or cellophane tape.

It is the practice in some shops to cover rollers with paper or cloth when a press is not in use, in order to limit exposure to light, since light—especially ultraviolet light—can shorten the life of a roller.

15

Paper

Selecting paper for letterpress printing

Most papers that print well with offset lithographic processes also print well with letterpress, provided that the surface of the paper is smooth, and not textured. Textures or finishes to avoid include laid and linen, which are made by pressing textured rollers over the surface to reform it, creating varying thicknesses of material. Offset presses, which use a rubber surface to transfer ink to the paper surface, can easily bend to fill the thousands of tiny valleys in these papers with ink, but the rigid surfaces used with letterpress cannot. When letterpress printers print on textured papers, they must use an exorbitant amount of pressure to equalize the impression over the undulating surface, and the type or plate is soon worn.

Paper quality

Paper is made from re-formed fibers, often with a coating to limit absorbency. Its qualities result from the maker's choice of fibers, the method of separating the fibers before re-forming, the method of re-forming, and the use of a coating or mechanical finish.

Paper has traditionally been made from linen or cotton fiber, and anyone interested in printing should study books made between the invention of moveable type in about 1450 until the early nineteenth century; the papers from that period are still strong and bright now. Linen and cotton have proven to be miraculous in their longevity.

In about 1860, wood fiber was intermingled with linen and cotton. While linen and cotton are naturally pure and stable, wood has inherent chemical properties that make it weaken and deteriorate with time. By 1890 or 1900, cotton and linen were components of special paper grades alone.

The self-destructive qualities of wood fiber can be mitigated chemically, however. Book publishers now produce mass-market hardcover books that are labeled "archival," though their paper consists entirely of wood fiber. But some people are skeptical of claims that any paper made from wood fiber can be long-lived.

Until the late eighteenth century, papermakers separated fibers from rags by rotting and beating them, typically with water-powered hammers. In about 1780, papermakers began *shredding* their fiber with a set of toothed rollers, called a hollander beater. The resulting fibers were shorter in length, and made a weaker paper, but the paper could be made more cheaply, in part because the rotting process could be eliminated.

There are, however, a handful of mills in the world that continue to produce paper from pounded, rather than shredded, fiber.

Paper density or "weight"

The old American system of measuring paper by the weight of 500 sheets of a standard basis size gave us everyday terms such as "20 lb. text" and "80 lb. cover." The latter terms will probably remain in use, but the complexities of the various basis sizes, which change according to the kind of paper, makes for inconsistent specifications for papers which are actually the same physical weight. Book papers, for example, are weighed as 500 sheets measuring 25 × 38 inches, while cover paper is measured as 500 sheets measuring 20 × 26 inches. The table below shows the results of this awkward system, in which a 40 lb. bond is the same density as a 100 lb. text, a 55 lb. cover, and a 67 lb. Bristol.

COMPARABLE PAPER WEIGHTS

Bond	Text	Cover	Bristol
20	50		
24	60		
28	70		
32	80		
40	100	55	67
	120	65	80
		80	100
		100	120

As a result, the more logical measurement of paper by grams per square meter is supplanting the old system.

With heavier stock, paper is sometimes identified by its actual thickness, using thousandths of an inch. This measure is sometimes specified in *points,* with 5 points being .005".

Buying paper

The letterpress printer may buy paper from commercial paper suppliers, art suppliers, and even hand paper-makers.

The commercial suppliers will have sample catalogs, sample rooms, and an inventory of the paper that they specialize in. The sample room staff is usually friendly and helpful, though their operation will naturally be oriented toward large lithographic printers that buy large quantities.

When buying from a commercial paper house, the printer should be prepared to purchase a good deal of paper, to pay with a credit card, and to wait several days for the paper to be received from the mill and cut by the merchant, if necessary. If the paper will eventually be resold, either as job work or art, the printer should be prepared to provide the needed paperwork so that retail sales tax can be avoided. The merchant will deliver the paper within a reasonable distance, but the details of this must be worked out in advance, as some merchants use large trucks that can't maneuver in residential neighborhoods, and may expect you to have a loading dock.

Paper that is popular is sometimes available in *broken lots,* and a printer can ask the merchant to package as few as 50 sheets. But the trend is increasingly toward selling intact cartons. If a paper isn't popular, the merchant may not keep any stock on hand, and you may have to wait while a carton is shipped from the mill.

Art paper is typically sold by the sheet, with small discounts for quantities of ten, twenty, 100, or 500 sheets. Art suppliers such as Utrecht, Daniel Smith, and Dick Blick stock a variety of printmaking papers that work well for letterpress, including some handmade papers from afar. For projects of high esthetic value, such as books, the art supplier is the best source of paper.

Dampening paper

An advantage of art paper is its increased ability to absorb impression and ink when dampened with water. All letterpress printing was done on dampened paper until about 1850.

Dampening increases the evenness of the ink and impression, increases the strength of the impression, and helps to accommodate the variations in the thickness of hand-made paper. I do all of my best printing by this method, though the preparation of the paper requires time.

Any method of dampening the paper will work, including immersion, sprinkling, sponging, or interleaving with blotters. It's essential to give the paper time to evenly absorb the water so that the sheets are dampened throughout, and all sheets are consistent in the amount of moisture they've absorbed. I immerse four or five sheets together in clean water, enclose them in a plastic tub, and let them sit overnight. When printing, I'm careful to remove only as many as I can use before they begin to dry out.

If I am printing both sides of a sheet, I will try to keep the sheets damp until the printing is done. When the printing is finished, I press them lightly with flat boards and weights as they dry, to prevent the sheets from cockling.

Dampening expands the paper slightly, and may frustrate later attempts to register printing previously done on the reverse side of a sheet, or a second color.

Good quality paper must be used. My attempts to print on various brands of dampened *commercial* paper, like that manufactured for office stationery, hasn't been successful, even though the paper is made entirely from cotton fiber. I suspect that the sizing isn't suitable for the process, but the problem may be the length of the fibers.

Counting paper

The stock for a project need not be counted individually, but can usually be estimated with sufficient exactness. Twenty-five sheets can be counted out, and a stack of similar height can be formed next to it. If the two are combined, the stack then contains fifty sheets, and if that stack is combined with another of comparable height, 100 sheets are at hand. This method will be accurate to within a few sheets per hundred.

If the project is typical, such accuracy is sufficient, especially since any printing process involves a certain amount of loss. Usually, an estimate of the loss is made and extra sheets are added to the stock to be printed. This is why commercial printing contracts stipulate that the quantity delivered will be within ten percent of the quantity ordered, and may be greater or lesser.

International, metric, or iso format system

In most of the world, paper is measured using a system of numbered sizes (such as "A3"), each half the size of the previous. The system was first adopted in Germany in the 1920s and was adopted in the Soviet Union in 1934, the U.K. in 1959, France in 1967, and Australia in 1974. The system is variously called the International, Metric, or ISO format system. Only the United States, Canada, and a few South American countries have failed to adopt it.

The base size A0 is one square meter in area. The proportions remain the same for all sizes, since each is based on a ratio in which the height divided by the width is the square root of two, or 1.4142.

Size A1, for example, is size A0 cut in half. The height of A1 is the width of A0, and the width of A1 is half the height of A0.

One advantage of the system is the ease with which designs can be reduced and enlarged from one paper size to another with perfectly-maintained proportions. Another is the efficiency with which paper can be converted from one size to another.

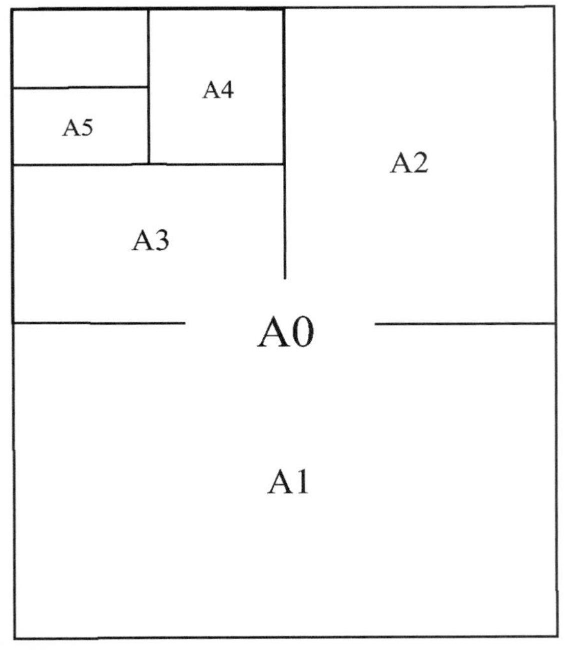

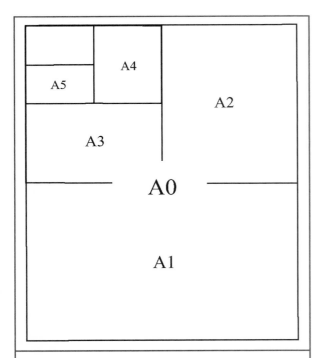

FIGURE 75
The ISO or metric "A series" paper sizes, showing the relationship between the various sizes of paper.

ISO "A" Series Paper Sizes

name	size in mm	size in inches
4A	1682 × 2378	66¼ × 93⅝
2A	1189 × 1682	46 13/16 × 66¼
A0	841 × 1189	33⅛ × 46 13/16
A1	594 × 841	23⅜ × 33⅛
A2	420 × 594	16½ × 23⅜
A3	297 × 420	11 11/16 × 16½
A4	210 × 297	8¼ × 11 11/16
A5	148 × 210	5 13/16 × 8¼
A6	105 × 148	4⅛ × 5 13/16
A7	74 × 105	2 15/16 × 4⅛
A8	53 × 74	2 13 16 × 2 15/16

A "B" series is also in use, with each numbered B size about 20 percent larger than the corresponding number in the A series. Paper in the B series is more friendly, since the base size, B0, is one meter in width. As a result, all of the large "B" sizes have one side that measures 125, 250, 500, 1,000, or 2,000 millimeters.

A "C" series is used to designate envelopes for the "A" series papers. A C6 envelope, for example, is designed to fit an A6 sheet. Since an A5 sheet, folded once, will equal the A6 sheet in size, it will also fit the C6 envelope. Any of the "A" series sheets, if folded a sufficient number of times, will fit any of the "C" series envelopes.

U.S. envelope sizes

A series of envelopes made in the U.S. for announcements, greeting cards, and invitations is numbered A2 through A10, a system which has nothing to do with the ISO or metric system discussed above. The A2 measures $4\frac{3}{8} \times 5\frac{3}{4}$ inches and the A10 measures $6 \times 9\frac{1}{2}$. A common $8\frac{1}{2} \times 11$ inch sheet will fit an A2 envelope when folded to $4\frac{1}{4}" \times 5\frac{1}{2}"$.

North American "A" Series Greeting Card Envelope Sizes

name	size in inches
A2	$4\frac{3}{8} \times 5\frac{3}{4}$
A6	$4\frac{3}{4} \times 6\frac{1}{2}$
A7	$5\frac{1}{4} \times 7\frac{1}{4}$
A8	$5\frac{1}{2} \times 8\frac{1}{8}$
A9	$5\frac{3}{4} \times 8\frac{3}{4}$
A10	$6 \times 9\frac{1}{2}$

Another "card" series is numbered 4 through 7, with size 7 sometimes called *Lee*. Some manufacturers call their envelopes *baronial* when the flap is pointed and *announcement* when the flap is square.

North American Baronial and Announcement Greeting Card Envelope Sizes

name	size in inches
$5\frac{1}{2}$	$4\frac{3}{8} \times 5\frac{3}{4}$
6	$4\frac{3}{4} \times 6\frac{1}{2}$
7 or Lee	$5\frac{1}{4} \times 7\frac{1}{4}$

Other manufacturers use the terms *baronial* and *announcement* to distinguish between two different series of envelope sizes, with the announcement series sized as in the table above, and the baronial in the following table:

Alternative North American Baronial Envelope Sizes

name	size in inches
2	$3\frac{3}{16} \times 4\frac{1}{4}$
4	$3\frac{5}{8} \times 4\frac{5}{8}$
5	$4\frac{1}{8} \times 5\frac{1}{8}$
$5\frac{1}{4}$	$4\frac{1}{4} \times 5\frac{1}{4}$
$5\frac{1}{2}$	$4\frac{3}{8} \times 5\frac{5}{8}$
6	$5 \times 6\frac{1}{4}$

In the United States and Canada, common business envelopes (called both *commercial* and *official*) are numbered, with the number 6¼ envelope measuring 3½ × 6 inches, the number 9 measuring 3⅞ × 8⅞, and the number 10 measuring 4⅛ × 9½. Some manufacturers call sizes 5 and 6¾ *commercial,* and sizes 7–14 *official.* The number 9 envelope is often used as a return envelope, and fits easily within the 10.

Most correspondence in North America is folded with two parallel folds, while correspondence elsewhere is folded with two perpendicular folds.

Cutting paper

It is much cheaper to purchase large sheets of paper rather than "cut sheets." Paper wholesalers once stocked thousands of different papers in local warehouses and would sell small amounts, but most now stock a small selection and order other papers in full cartons or *carton lots,* which are ordered from the mill as needed. Cartons usually contain 1,000 sheets of paper, roughly 2 × 3 feet.

Paper merchants, binderies, and commercial printers will cut stock for you, often for a dollar or two per cut. But you will find that having a paper cutter is quite useful, even if it's limited in size. Regardless of your cutting equipment, a combination of in-house and outside cutting is often practical. The printer orders a carton, has the wholesaler cut it to a size that can be handled on the shop's largest press, and then cuts down the stock in-house as needed for individual projects.

When planning a project, one can often divide a large sheet into many equal parts to obtain the final sheet size; the entire sheet is used.

But sometimes the finished size is fixed, for example, when a business card is to be 2 × 3½ inches. Then the paper is simply cut to that size and the waste discarded.

To minimize waste, determine how the sheet is best divided. Take the dimensions of the large sheet and divide these by the two dimensions of the finished sheet to find the number of finished sheets that the large sheet will yield. If the same calculation is made with one set of dimensions in a different order, a comparison of the results will indicate which cutting pattern yields the greatest number of finished sheets.

For example, I designed a greeting card for some baronial style envelopes I had on hand; a 6¾ × 10¼ inch card, folded once, fit the envelope nicely. I was cutting from sheets of 23 × 35 inch paper, and the math looked like this:

$$23 \div 6\tfrac{3}{4} = 3 \qquad 35 \div 10\tfrac{1}{4} = 3$$
3 from the width, 3 from the length $\qquad 3 \times 3 = 9$

$$35 \div 6\tfrac{3}{4} = 5 \qquad 23 \div 10\tfrac{1}{4} = 2$$
5 from the length, 2 from the width $\qquad 5 \times 2 = 10$

It's not necessary to carry the result beyond whole numbers, since we're interested only in the number of whole pieces each division will yield.

When cutting, it is usually best to preserve as many of the original edges as possible, because the cutting machinery at the mill or warehouse is usually better than the machinery in the small shop, and the angles will be more accurate. But sometimes the edges are soiled or battered, and one must cut them off and discard them.

When you are cutting stock down and the finished sheets must be consistent in size, make rough cuts, and then set the cutter once for each of the final cuts, running all the stock through the cutter before readjusting the machine.

Paper cutters

There are two styles of paper cutters: guillotine and shear. For some inexplicable reason, the public has begun to call shear style cutters "guillotines."

A guillotine style lowers a wide, heavy blade in a vertical frame onto a stack of paper that is clamped to the bed of the cutter. These typically cut as much paper as can be placed under the clamp. They are made in many sizes, with bed widths from about 18 inches to 60 inches. Above 30 inches, they are usually powered. Some smaller models are designed for a tabletop or bench.

A shear style (or lever-knife) cutter uses a hand-held lever combined with a blade. It can cut only a handful of sheets at a time. Many sizes are made, up to about 36×36 inches.

I have both styles in my shop; the guillotine style for cutting paper to size for printing, and the shear style for cutting a few sheets for proofing, for preparing packing and tympan paper, and other odd jobs.

Heavy shear cutters, called board shears, are made to cut binder's board for book binding and box making. They are difficult to use with paper. Binder's board is said to contain metallic remnants that will dull or nick a cutting blade. For this reason, many printers avoid cutting it on their paper cutters.

Maintenance: shears

For safety, the spring at the fulcrum of the blade should be tight enough to hold the blade aloft on its own. The fulcrum should be kept oiled, and the board surface should be kept clean. The operator should ascertain if the ruler is accurate; often the grid tooled on the board is a better guide than the ruler. The ruler can usually be adjusted.

The upper guide on the cutter must be square with the steel edge on the lever side. A T-square or carpenter's square will be helpful to test the squareness of the paper; a carpenter's square will be helpful to adjust the guide.

Maintenance: guillotine cutters

Cutters should be oiled frequently, sharpened occasionally, and tuned up from time to time.

Oil holes are usually provided for oil, and oil or grease can be carefully applied to the bearing surface against which the blade head slides.

When needed, the blade can be sharpened on a bench with a file and leather strop. If the blade is in poor condition, a professional sharpening service will make it right. When the blade is removed from the cutter, a wood shipping case will protect the edge of the blade and make it safe to handle. Sharpening services provide placards marked "sharp" and "dull," which are useful for shops storing several blades.

On a guillotine cutter, the blade comes to rest against a cutting stick made of maple or plastic which lies in a groove in the bed. Eventually the stick will dent and the bottom-most sheets won't cut well, but then the stick can be rotated until all four sides are used.

The cutter must occasionally be *squared,* or adjusted so that the blade cuts squarely across the paper. For cutting, the paper rests against the side and back gauge of the cutter; the back gauge is usually adjusted by loosening a few bolts.

A carpenter's framing square can be used to adjust the back gauge and make it nearly square. A final test is made by dropping the blade onto the middle of a large sheet of paper whose edges are square. The sheet needn't be clamped, but can be stabilized with a hand if necessary. With the blade, crease the paper without cutting it, remove it from the bed, and fold it at the crease. The squareness will be indicated by the manner in which the ends line up.

If a carpenter's square isn't available, the folding method alone can be used.

The blade's contact with the cutting stick should also be square, with both the right and left sides touching down at the same time.

The bed, gauge, and clamp surfaces should be kept clean and free of rust.

Operation: guillotine cutters

The measuring tapes on many cutters aren't reliable, including the one in my shop. To set up the cutter, I lower the blade directly onto a wood yardstick which I hold against the back gauge.

With the back gauge set to the proper distance from the blade edge, the paper is placed on the bed and jogged against the side and back gauge. A block of clean wood can be used to strike the sides of the pile for jogging. If the blade travels from right to left as it descends, place the stack against the left side. Lower the clamp until the stack is held tightly, but avoid excessive pressure. Lower the blade with an even stroke until the stack is cut. Lift the blade and raise the clamp.

Paper will tear slightly on the unclamped side of the blade, making a comparatively rough edge. If the blade is sharp and the cutting stick good, the effect isn't noticeable.

Normally the clamp will dent several sheets on the top of the stack and make them unusable, and the bed will soil the bottom-most sheet. With each cut, these sheets must be inspected and removed from the stack. If the paper is sandwiched between sheets of chipboard before cutting, these problems will be avoided.

Keep tools off of the bed. Pens, pencils, and rulers are easily lost among the paper and will damage the blade. It is best to form a habit of *never* placing them on the bed. On my cutter, I use a wood yardstick without any metal fixtures; its extra length makes it difficult to overlook when cutting, and its relative softness will prevent serious damage if the blade does contact it.

The clamp exerts a lot of pressure, and care must be taken that ink doesn't transfer onto neighboring sheets. I try to cut paper before printing whenever possible. On the press, it's rather simple to produce perfect margins and get things square. On a cutter, minor mistakes can ruin an entire job.

Because the blade is very sharp and there is typically a lot of hand movement around it, the guillotine paper cutter is one of the most dangerous tools in the shop. If the cutter is not equipped with a counterweight or catch to keep the blade from falling, one should be improvised. On many cutters the bottom of the clamp rests below the level of the blade edge when it's at rest in the "up" position, protecting the operator from accidental contact with the blade. But on some cutters, the clamp can be raised above the blade, exposing it completely. If the clamp on a particular machine *can* rise above the blade, the printer should form the habit of raising the clamp short of the blade edge and not above it. A wood stop can be placed on the clamp to regulate its travel.

Serious cuts can result when operators manually tear paper upward against the clamp and accidentally contact the blade. Tearing of this kind is usually done because the cutter needs maintenance and the blade is scoring, rather than cutting, some of the sheets.

Irregular sizes and registration

Occasionally, you may work with stock that is irregular in size, or that contains previously-printed material in varying position to which your work must register. A printmaker, for example, may ask you to add a title and caption to several copies of an etching which was printed in various positions on the stock. Registration is still possible, though the process is slow and tedious. The first method, involving pins, will adjust the position along two axes; the second method, involving feeding marks, can adjust the position along only one axis.

Pins are an ancient method of positioning and holding a sheet on the press. The pins can be made from thumbtacks with thin heads, which are taped to the tympan or pushed through it from the platen or cylinder side. The sheet is mounted on them. If pins were used for the first printing, the work is simple. Otherwise, the pins must be positioned in relation to some feature of the printing that is already on the sheet. One method is to use a light table and a guide to stab the sheet with a pin in positions that correspond with the pins on the press. Typically, the pin holes are later burnished closed or trimmed away from the sheet. If the pins pierce the sheet along a fold, which is preferable for book work, the pin holes can be left.

Alternatively, the stock can be fed to a mark. The top of the sheet is fed to the grippers or gauge pins, but the edge of the sheet, normally so important in feeding a press, is ignored, and the center or margin of the printing is lined up to a mark made on the cylinder or platen. For precise registration, a mylar sheet is marked to correspond with some feature of the existing printing and made to be positioned with the side guide and grippers. With the sheet below the mylar guide and the mylar held in place against the side guide and grippers, the sheet is moved sideways on the press until registered with the marks on the mylar. Once positioned, the sheet is held firmly to the feed table or platen while the mylar guide is removed. On a cylinder press, the sheet can be adjusted slightly if the marks on the mylar show the existing printing on the sheet to be crooked. On a platen press, the sheet can be adjusted and stuck to the tympan with a bit of tape.

Synthetic papers

A number of synthetic papers have been introduced in the last decade or two, which are perfect for outdoor or marine use. Polyart (made by Arjobex) is a clay-coated polyethylene film. Hop-syn (made by Hop Industries Corporation) is a calendered mixture of clay and polypropylene. Teslin (made by PPG) is an unspecified polyolefin, with 60% of its weight coming from filler and 65% of its volume from air. Tyvek (made by Dupont) consists of polyethylene fibers without filler.

The manufacturers of Polyart, Tyvek, Teslin, and Hop-syn indicate that their product is suited for letterpress printing with standard inks.

Handling the completed job

Once printed, most sheets can be stacked directly on top of one another, and even jogged to even the edges of the stack. If large areas of the sheet are covered with ink, however, a *slip sheet* should be inserted between each printed sheet to prevent the ink from *setting-off* or soiling the neighboring sheet. Clean, unprinted paper is best for slip sheeting, but newspaper can be used in a pinch. If the ink coverage is excessive, the sheets can be hung by clothespins on a line to dry, placed in a drying rack, or laid out on tables. Drier can also be added to the ink; its use is discussed in the section on ink.

When the ink has dried so that it can't be smeared with a finger, the job may be wrapped in paper. It is a nice touch to paste a printed sheet on the top of the wrapper to indicate what's inside.

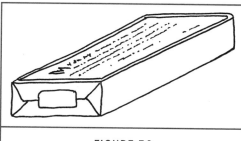

FIGURE 76
A printed job wrapped in paper.
An example is pasted to the top.

16

Hand Washing & Clothing

Hand washing

Even in a relatively clean shop, the printer's hands are soon covered with dirt, oil, and ink after contact with "unclean" things, such as type and machinery. Any paper handled will be marked with soil unless the hands are clean, especially if the stock is hand-fed to a press.

Very small amounts of ink and oil can be removed from the hands with a rag and talc. The usual procedure for serious filth is to wipe the hands with a rag, scrub them with strong soap or hand cleaner, and towel them dry. If wanted, a dusting of talc can be used to dry any remaining oil or ink.

Ordinary soap will not remove ink and oil. The printer must find a hand cleaner or soap that is strong, yet mild enough not to chap the hands with repeated use. I have been pleased with handmade soap, a few commercial soaps such as Lava, and commercial hand cleaners containing orange oil (also known as Limonene, d-Limonene or l-Limonene), including the orange product made by Go-Jo. Some printers report good results with mineral oil or baby oil, and waterless soap purchased from an auto supply store.

Hand cleaner must be washed away with soap and water. If no plumbing is available in the shop, a wash basin can be used.

To test whether the hands are really clean, the fingers can be rubbed across the surface of a toothy sheet of white paper. This method will also work to partially clean a small amount of ink off of the hands.

Hand washing is also an important technique to prevent the ingestion of lead, a subject discussed in the chapter on safety.

Clothing

For safety reasons, I discourage the wearing of aprons around machines, and simply encourage printers to wear tight fitting clothes they can sully.

My college printmaking instructor declared that ink on clothing never comes out in the wash, "it just gets cleaner." But I have since learned that ink can be laundered away if a laundry stain stick or stain remover is applied before the ink sets.

Since printers tend to move heavy materials with some frequency, I recommend every printer own a pair of steel toed boots. They will last nearly forever, and will pay for themselves the first time you or a fellow worker drop something heavy on your foot.

17

Editing, Orthography, & Proofreading

Basic editing and proofreading

The letterpress printer must sometimes function as an editor, and should know the rudiments of reading, correcting, and proofreading text for publication.

There are two stages in converting a manuscript into type that is ready for printing:

1. Editing the manuscript. This is best done by someone with extensive experience in reading and writing. Editing can be simple copy editing, to check spelling and mechanics, it can be a more extensive review of organization, style, sense and language, and it can be a full study of the work, including verification of references and entries in a bibliography.
2. Proofreading the galley proofs. This is best done by two people: one who reads the manuscript aloud while another follows through the printed proof. Proofreading is done to check the proof for omissions and departures from the manuscript.

An editor must have at hand reference books that show the preferred style for mechanical matters, including spelling, capitalization, and punctuation. Many publishers use the *Chicago Manual of Style* and Webster's *Dictionary* as their authorities. If the material is lengthy, and specialized words are used, the editor may prepare an additional list of words to ensure that the author is using and spelling words consistently. If the manuscript is being edited on a computer, the spell-checking function can accomplish this.

Someone other than the person who set the type should examine the proofs. This is especially important if the material has been written by the compositor, as the eyes of the compositor and reader often see what they wish to see, rather than what is in the type or on the page. Never proofread your own stuff.

Proofreaders should be familiar with proofreading marks, and use them consistently, so that the typesetter understands clearly what needs to be changed. Several versions of these marks exist, and the proofreaders and typesetters should agree on which system is used.

It is more than a courtesy for an editor to submit all changes in a manuscript to the author for approval. The accuracy of the final text depends on it.

Some proofreaders find it fruitful to read copy backwards, one word at a time, to check for spelling errors. When reading backwards, it is impossible to make sense of the text, and the proofreader's concentration is devoted to each word as an individual unit.

A superb guide that addresses common errors in mechanics and style is *The Elements of Style,* by William Strunk Jr. and E.B. White.

Six poorly-understood typographical protocols

EM DASH, AND EN DASH An em dash is a long dash, about an em long, used to separate phrases. A short dash, about an en long, is used to join words. The typographical treatment of the em dash varies, but a thin space—perhaps a five to the em space—is best placed on either side of an em dash. No space is used around an en dash. It is confusing when short dashes are mistakenly substituted for long dashes, as they have opposite influences on the reader.

> *This diabolical person—who, by the way, I didn't know—claimed to be my brother.*
> *I was struck by the inward-facing woodwork.*

PUNCTUATION INSIDE QUOTATIONS In North America, punctuation should always be placed inside quotation marks. Exceptions are the colon and semi-colon, which most authorities believe should be placed outside quotation marks. The practice differs in Britain, so confusion here is understandable. In Britain, punctuation is placed within quotation marks only when it belongs to the original; the style is sometimes called "logical," since the placement of the punctuation signals whether it is from the original or not. A growing movement in North America supports the logical style.

ELLIPSIS POINTS Ellipsis points signal omissions within a quote or transcription. They are formed with three periods separated by three thin spaces, perhaps four-to-the-em; they are not placed side by side. If the material that is omitted follows a period in the original, the period is left intact, and appears before the ellipsis in its normal place.

> *I knew everything. But I didn't know much. I basically knew nothing at all.*
>
> *I knew everything. . . . I basically knew nothing at all.*

IT'S AND ITS English forms the possessive by adding an apostrophe or an apostrophe and an 's', but the word *its* is an exception. The contraction of the words *it is,* however, is *it's.*

> *It's unfortunate, but its odor was driving her nuts.*

Other words that aren't written with an apostrophe are: *ours, yours, hers,* and *his.*

The apostrophe seems to be disappearing, though the British have formed the Apostrophe Protection Society to prevent this.

STATE ABBREVIATIONS Twenty years ago, the U.S. Postal Service asked us to substitute two-letter codes for the traditional abbreviations used for states; they also asked us to write the *entire* address in upper case letters, which was less confusing to the optical scanners that were being introduced to sort mail. While the use of upper case letters was never widely adopted, the state abbreviations now infect our typography, despite their ugliness and the confusion they present by appearing to be acronyms.

> *According to the TV, the UN has an office in MN.*

Nearly anything is better than writing "MN," including "Mn.," and "Minn." It is mass psychosis to abandon names so historically rich and graceful as "Massachusetts" or "Maine" for "MA" or "ME" in formal text. Nearly all style books call for traditional abbreviations for states ("Minn., Mass."), with a handful of states (such as "Ohio") spelled out.

TIME OF DAY The time of day is divided by noon into two parts: before noon (*ante* meridiem, or "A.M.") and after noon (*post* meridiem, or "P.M."). It is not logical to call noon, a point in time which divides A.M. and P.M., "12 P.M.," which would mean "noon after noon." Noon is 12 noon.

Midnight divides the days, and like noon, is an instant in time. It is properly called "12 midnight," or simply "midnight." It is not logical to call midnight "12 A.M."

18

Planning the Project

Designing the project

Before you set the first line of type, you must determine the line length that you will use. Choosing ten, fifteen, or twenty picas is convenient, because standard furniture lengths will correspond nicely to a block of type of that width. But it is an easy thing to build up a block of type 13 picas in width, for example, with a few slugs on each side of the form, and bring the type block to 15 picas, or an *even measure*.

Most printing projects begin with rough sketching and a little experimentation with the probable size of paper to be used.

Design by proof

While all graphic processes have some means of proofing designs before printing, proofing is most faithful for the hand printer working in lithography, intaglio, and letterpress.

In these traditional printmaking methods, a preliminary design is enhanced and proofed until the work reaches a final state. Subtle interactions of color, tone, and visual effect can be taken into account as the design is brought forward.

I strongly urge letterpress students to exploit the same proofing process to inform their design decisions as they set type. This principle is discussed more fully in the chapter titled "Proofing type."

Mock-ups and prototypes

A mock-up is a crude model of a printed piece, sometimes made to experiment with various paper stocks or printed designs. A prototype is a more finished example of a project, often used to test binding styles and the usability of paper work such as fold-outs, pop-ups, tabs, enclosures, etc.

It is wise to test a design which may be unfamiliar to the user by distributing five or six prototypes to friends and listening to their comments after some time has passed. Problems with paper work can be discovered and corrected by observing if a design remains intact after being handled by several people.

Type

If a text is to be set into type by hand, the printer should make certain that he or she will not run out of sorts. To *cast off copy* is to estimate how much type will be required to set a manuscript, or how many pages it will fill when set. Tables in type specimen books are available for these estimates.

Sort Snorter, a Microsoft Word macro written by Mark Wilden and available on the web, counts the number of each sort required for a particular document, and the number can be compared to what is available in the case.

If the type is to be set by machine, the printer needn't worry; the machine is designed to make as many sorts as needed.

If setting by hand and machine, you should be sure that any unusual characters are available.

Many printers draw their basic layout before beginning, experimenting with different faces or fonts. It is also possible to experiment by setting and proofing a few lines of type.

Paper size

Unless the process prevents it, cut the paper to its finished size *after* designing and *before* printing. When cutting is done before printing, final positioning is more assured, and you avoid set-off, or the transfer of ink from one sheet to another, from the pressure of the clamp on the cutter. You also avoid idiotic cutting mistakes. It is disagreeable to remove a project from the cutter and realize that, because half of it was oriented upside down in the pile, you have just trimmed the top of half the sheets and the bottom of the other half.

More information on cutting is given in the chapter titled "Paper."

How many to print?

If a printed item is to be sold, estimate the probable number of sales by talking with others in the field and by surveying prospects. Most artists and publishers make the greatest number of sales during the year following the creation of a project, and sales then dwindle with time. Some prefer to sell out a title or piece within a year or two and move on. The temptation of the beginner is to print too many.

The kind of press being used will determine the practical size of an edition. As a general rule, a hand press will comfortably print editions of ten to a hundred, a hand cylinder press will print editions numbering in the hundreds, a powered platen press will print thousands, and an automatically fed and powered press of any kind will print tens of thousands.

Hand folding and hand binding are the most troublesome part of a project; it is common to underestimate the amount of drudgery involved and the time required. The temptation is to bind only half of a printed edition, in the hope that future sales will oblige one to bind the second half. Most of us have a difficult time finding the time and energy to resume the binding work after newer, more exciting projects are forged. As a result, we cease marketing the already printed project, and we forgo the sale of the unbound half. In the end, we would have saved ourselves time and expense by printing a smaller number.

Mailing

If the finished piece is to be individually mailed, be certain that it conforms to postal rules and preferences. Staples are shunned because they cut the carrier's hands when they reach into their bags, and there is a preferred method of folding so that a piece feeds properly through processing machinery. There are extra charges for mail that is not rectangular, and mail that exceeds standard dimensions (including thickness) and weight. There are also minimum sizes for mail. The current minimum size in the U.S. is 3 ½ inches high by 5 inches wide; the maximum for first class rates without surcharge is 6⅛ high × 11½ wide × ¼ thick. Cards, if they are to be mailed at card rates, have the same minimum (3½ inches high × 5 inches wide), but a different maximum (4¼ inches high × 6 inches wide).

The post office can provide a printed guide, and for those who are "type A" personalities, there is a regularly published *Domestic Mail Manual* that rivals a large phone book in size. Your local post office may give you an older copy when a new version is issued; the DMM is also available on the internet.

I often design a printed piece and bring a proof or a mock-up to the local post office for review, especially if it's intended to be mailed under bulk rate rules, which are more restrictive than those for regular mail. Bulk rate rules reserve part of the address panel for postal service markings, for example. By sharing your design with the post office staff you may also learn that some widely-held notions are misconceptions. At one organization, the staff was able to save a lot of time in preparing a two-fold mailing when we learned that it didn't have to be bound together with adhesive tabs, as everyone seems to think.

Two rates that printers should know about are "bound printed matter" (for advertising, editorial, and directory material) and "media mail" for books.

Envelopes, folding and blanks

If the piece will be inserted into an envelope, make sure there's plenty of room for it to fit. If the piece is to be folded, work with a finished example

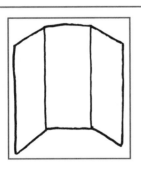

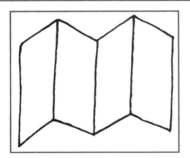

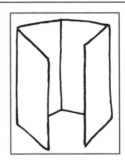

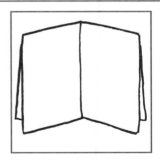

C Fold
Also known as a letterfold, number 10 fold, three panel fold, brochure fold, and the misleading "trifold." The panel which swings inside should be narrower than the other panels.

Accordion Fold
Panels fold on top of each other like an accordion.

Gate Fold
The two end panels fold inward. The end panels must be narrower than the two interior panels.

French Fold
The sheet is folded in half, then in half again with a perpendicular fold. Also called a right-angle fold.

FIGURE 77
Common folds.

or mock-up; do not design solely in your head. Check that folds do not interfere with readability or appearance. If the folding is to be sent out to another shop, consult with the shop's staff and design the project for the preferred sequence of folds.

If the piece contains blank lines that the user is expected to fill in, make sure there's ample space to fit long names, long addresses, etc., by having a few people try out the form. Form designers, in general, should be aware of social trends: people are now combining their surname with that of their spouse, for example, and individuals often have three phone numbers.

Paper quantity

Some amount of paper will be ruined on the press, and it is wise to prepare about 10 percent more paper than will be needed for a project. If the job will be run through the press more than once, then at least 10 percent more should be added for each run.

Some complicated projects with multiple press passes will result in more waste than normal. It is inefficient to run short of finished sheets and be forced to prepare the paper, form, and press again for printing from the beginning. Print an ample amount during the initial press run, even though this may result in having to discard some of the sheets.

When projects require work after the initial press run, such as scoring or additional printing, any ruined sheets should be kept on hand for setting up the next process. They should be kept separate from the good sheets at all times.

Paper grain

The majority of the fibers in a machine-made paper are oriented in a particular direction called the *grain*. For booklets and books, the grain should run parallel to the vertical axis of the book as it sits on a shelf; that is, the grain should point up and down. This convention provides the greatest strength along the axis which has the greatest stress, and prevents the book from changing shape with time.

Some papers fold awkwardly against the grain, and if a job is to be folded, the grain direction may affect the design. Scoring or creasing will allow most papers to be folded.

To test for grain, turn one part of a sheet of paper over another part, as though you are about to fold the sheet in half, and press lightly on the surface above the roll which forms in the middle of the sheet. Try the sheet in one direction and then in the other: one roll will be more yielding. The direction or axis of that roll lies parallel to the fibers, or grain.

Grain is created on the paper-making machine as the paper fibers orient themselves in the direction of the flow while the pulp moves onto the screen. The screen is shaken sidewise to reorient the fibers and reduce the amount of grain. Handmade paper has virtually no grain because the pulp is picked up from a vat with a hand-held screen, and the screen is shaken in several directions.

On labels and in catalogs the dimension of the sheet that lies parallel to the grain is often underlined. A sheet described as "22 × 30" has its grain direction parallel to its 30 inch edge.

General design

It is widely accepted that the visual center of a rectangle is centered between the side margins, but is slightly higher than the actual midpoint between the top and bottom. As a result, more margin should be placed below the printing than above. An appealing effect is obtained by making the bottom margin the largest, and making the top and side margins of equal size.

I have noticed that type which is laid out *architecturally,* with a form that would be stable if the letters were blocks that were physically stacked upon each other, is usually more pleasing than type that is laid out so that it would be unstable.

Book design

Through long experience, printers have developed a pattern for positioning type on the pages of books. The pattern calls for:
1. an ample margin at the tail, both to create space to hold the book, and to create a pleasing visual effect.
2. an ample margin in the gutter, so that the printed matter is restricted to the part of the page which lies flat, and is isolated visually from the text on the facing page.
3. an ample margin at the fore-edge, to create space to hold the book
4. ample margins all around, to provide excess in case the book should be rebound and re-trimmed.
5. a relationship between the gutter, fore-edge, and head and tail that creates a visual balance. The gutter margin, which is in effect doubled, should not amount to more than the fore-edge margin.

When a printed sheet is to be folded into a book or a gathering for a book, the printer must take care to design the margins to account for the binding, the trimming, and for *margin creep.*

Most bindings trap some of the folded edge of each gathering within the spine, reducing the amount of gutter margin that is seen in the finished book by the reader. The printer must understand how much paper will be held by the binding, and allow for this loss. Some binding styles will absorb a considerable amount of the gutter margin. Nonetheless, the book should be designed so that the text lies only on the level plane of the page when the book is opened flat, and none of the text runs off the page and into the gutter.

The block of paper that forms a book is usually trimmed while being bound, and an allowance must be made for the loss at the head, tail, and fore-edge.

Margin creep or *wrap around* refers to the loss of gutter margin that appears in the outer portion of the signature. Because the outermost sheets must wrap around the inner sheets, their gutter margins must be enlarged to allow for the extra bulk of the inner pages. If an allowance isn't made, the position of the type will vary from page to page. With small gatherings of sheets, the variability won't be noticeable, but with signatures containing eight or more sheets, the difference will be pronounced.

These potential problems should be addressed in a mock-up of the book, using the same paper planned for the finished work. If a bookbinder is involved in the project, he or she can be consulted for advice.

FIGURE 78
Traditional proportions for a book layout.
The gutter margins lie next to the fold;
the fore-edge margins at the right and left
sides; the head at the top;
and the tail at the bottom.

Logic

Most printers agree that text should flow logically, and most work to avoid awkward divisions in their text. These include a *widow,* a short line at the top of the page, especially one consisting of one or two words. Other *bad breaks* are heads or sub-heads that appear at or near the bottom of the page. These things are avoided by manipulating the number of lines in the preceding pages, or by altering either the preceding white space or the text itself.

Beauty

Many fine press printers adhere fervently to "rules" that are really manifestations of taste. Some are concerned that each line in a book lines up perfectly with the lines on the reverse side of the sheet. Some fret about punctuation at the end of lines, and *hang* it slightly out in the margin to make the right edge of the text block look even. Some work to eliminate "rivers of white" created by the spaces between words that flow visually down the page. Among printers, those trained in colleges and universities adhere most forcefully to the rules they were taught, and regard them as flawless tenets of the art, rather than as elements of an artistic style.

It is instructive for every printer to reflect on why they believe in their own rules. Are they, in fact, someone else's rules, dutifully embraced from a mentor, rather than from personal admiration of the result? Do they actually result in more beautiful printing?

Some typographical suggestions

Some typographical effects created automatically by computers have resulted in greater ugliness, rather than greater elegance. It will benefit beginning letterpress printers to observe some of the traditional aspects of design and compare them to the machine-controlled practices of today.

If you are using a computer to generate text for printing, awareness is especially important. You must recognize the typographical changes embedded in the new technology and study their characteristics, and then make your own decisions about how the text should appear on the page. If you're not satisfied with the decisions the machine is making for you, the next step is to find the means of controlling the machine, which is often frustrating and time-consuming.

Legibility

"Only your wildest ingenuity," said Beatrice Warde, "can stop people from reading a really interesting text."

In the best graphic design, the textual message and the blending of shapes and color is seamless and legibility is superb. An understanding of where to approach the text is quickly conveyed: the printed piece is convenient. The worst graphic design obscures the textual message, impedes reading speed, or challenges the reader's sense of orientation. None of these

MODERN AND TRADITIONAL TYPOGRAPHY

	MODERN	TRADITIONAL
apostrophe:	'	'
quotation:	" "	" "
ligatures:	ff fi ffi fl ffl	ff fi ffi fl ffl
kerning:	Way.	Way.
emphasis:	Emphasis.	*Emphasis.*

space following punctuation:

White space is good. Let's use it.   White space is good. Let's use it.

set width variation used to justify columns:

White space is good. Let's use it.   White space is good. Let's use it.

A TRADITIONAL METHOD of arranging an "initial letter" in a block of type. When the letters 'A,' 'D,' 'O,' 'L,' and 'Q' are used as initial letters, the body of the initial letter must be mortised to allow the following letters to lie near the letterform. If this is not done, they will not appear to be connected.

FIGURE 79
Modern and traditional typography.

defects are welcomed by the reader, no matter how novel the design.

Traditional letterpress involved a series of constraints affecting spacing and orientation of the text. Suddenly released from these constraints, our culture is entering a period when typographical trends appear to be making text more difficult, rather than more efficient, to read. The relaxed letter spacing inherent in metal type has been squeezed out of the page, with letters sometimes kerned against each other according to how closely they can fit. Changes in the whole appearance of words has resulted, requiring readers to redefine the mental catalogue of shapes they use to identify words.

In the past, the reader has traditionally been rewarded with a visual pause between sentences, equivalent perhaps to the temporal pause made when speaking or reading aloud. The smallest punctuation mark, the period, does the most crucial work: it separates sentences into discrete units. To do this, the puny period must be made conspicuous by succeeding white space that allows easy recognition as the end of the sentence is approached. Use copious space between sentences, and between parts of a sentence separated by colons and semi-colons.

All letterpress printers will benefit from a study of typography before the late twentieth century, when most text was set in metal type. It was an extremely graceful period, when printers clearly strove to provide easy access to their text.

Maintaining a record of materials

A printer will sometimes want to know what type, paper, or ink was used for one of his or her own projects in the past. Fellow printers will sometimes ask about the details of a project years after it's completed; more often, you yourself will wish to re-use the type, paper, or ink, and will want to have the details: the maker, size, and name of type; the maker, type, and color of ink; and the maker, name, weight, color, surface texture, size, and grain direction of paper.

Some book printers include information about the paper and type in a colophon, a traditional statement which gives details on the design and printing. A colophon is usually placed at the end of the book. Others make a handwritten record in a copy of the book that they retain. In my own work, I often cut the label from a carton of paper that I will likely order again and tack it to the wall.

19

Special Processes

Reviving worn type

Some flaws of debilitated type can be corrected by the printer. Type which has counters that are filled with dried ink can sometimes be restored by picking the ink from the counters with a sewing pin, using care not to scratch the face of the type. Solvents such as acetone may also be used to soften or dissolve dried ink. Type which is worn can often be made to print by overlaying individual sorts. Type which is poorly lined, with the baseline of the characters badly aligned, can sometimes be bent into place with an awl or heavy needle, but the type must be relatively small, say 12 points and smaller. With larger type that is poorly lined, strips of paper or cardboard can be laid into the form at the top or bottom edges of the sorts, as needed, to bring the characters into alignment.

Printing on envelopes

Printing return addresses on envelopes can be challenging when the various layers of paper—including the flap—overlap to form a printing surface that varies in thickness. There are three approaches.

The simplest solution is to seek out envelopes that are cut with relatively large areas of uniform thickness in the upper corners, usually with full or nearly full flaps, and with glued overlaps on the back that are narrow. A *side-seam* envelope has its overlaps near the sides.

The most tedious and least satisfactory solution is to place overlays on the tympan or in the press packing to make up the difference in thickness. The overlays are usually made by cutting an envelope apart, so that they are the proper thickness. It is difficult and time-consuming to align the overlays, as three variations in thickness are usually involved, and any slight change in register while printing will spoil the result, possibly damaging the type as well.

The third solution is to place the return address on the flap of the envelope, printing each envelope with the flap opened. Any envelope can be printed in this way.

Many different sizes and styles of envelope are manufactured, and most any paper can be made into envelopes by shops known as envelope converters. Craft and scrapbook shops also sell equipment for converting paper into envelopes by hand.

Line art

Drawings and other line art can be converted to a relief printing surface by the photoengraving or photopolymer processes described earlier, or by carving a surface by hand. The hand method gives the line a unique appearance that nicely complements type.

If working with photographic processes, ensure that the shop preparing the photographic work doesn't apply a halftone screen when there are no greys that require screening, for example, when you are reproducing pure line art or a wood-engraving.

Photographs

Photographs can be printed on letterpress equipment from type-high photoengravings, though the results are not very satisfactory. The engravings are actually etchings made by reducing parts of the plate with acid, described in the section on photoengraving above. In the past, photoengravings were etched into copper, which prints much more readily and faithfully than magnesium, the material in use today. Unfortunately, copper photoengravings are no longer available.

In order to be printed with ink, a photograph must first be screened or made into a *halftone*. This is because ink is monochromatic, while a photograph contains a large variety of gray tones.

First, a negative is made with a halftone screen, which converts the blacks and grays into variously sized dots according to their intensity. A solid black when viewed through the screen will form large dots, a gray of medium intensity will form dots of medium size, and solid white will form no dots.

Halftone screens are designated by the number of dots created in a linear inch. The screens are rated in lines, because lines were once engraved or etched on glass to create the screen. A 90 line screen will make printing very easy, but will be rather rough in appearance when printed; letterpress halftones can be printed up to about 150 lines per inch.

Halftone plates are quick to fill with ink and debris. Printing from halftone plates should be done on glossy, coated paper, which will be more forgiving and will not generate as many pickings, or minute pieces of fiber that are torn from the paper surface by the plate.

Carved surfaces

Letterpress printers will find their work well-complemented with hand carved surfaces. Images may be cut into linoleum, wood, and a few newly available plastics such as Flexi-cut, Soft-kut, E-z-Cut, and Plasticut.

Wood is usually obtained type high, but linoleum and plastic will often be sold unmounted. The mounting can be done with ¾″ board, using either small nails or an adhesive such as carpenter's glue.

When carving any of this material, the work will be easier if the material is first mounted, and a bench hook is used to steady the block.

If a linoleum block is warmed slightly, on a radiator, hot plate, or even with a hair dryer, it will be softer and easier to cut. The tool will slip, so both hands should remain clear; cut so that the tool is never pointed toward any part of the body, and keep the tool sharp. You need not cut deeply, perhaps an eighth or a sixteenth of an inch. You might protect the surface of the block against errant wanderings of the tool

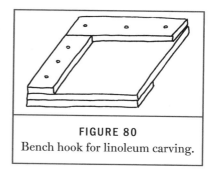

FIGURE 80
Bench hook for linoleum carving.

by masking the surface with a piece of wood nailed to the bench hook. Work the tool slowly, cutting a small amount at a time. If a consistently thick line is sought, cut the inside of its curves first, then bring the cutting in from the outside. Sharpening one's cutting tools is just as important as the cutting itself. The project should start with a thorough sharpening of tools, and the work should be interrupted with repeated bouts of re-sharpening. To reduce large areas of a block, use a large chisel.

Linoleum which is mounted by the manufacturer is usually not type high, but requires a little light card stock to bring it up. Linoleum eventually becomes hardened with time.

It may be impossible to print a block with a large printing area along with type, because the ink density required for the two surfaces is so different.

There are several methods of transferring a drawing to a block. The drawing can be traced onto its own back, and the drawing, now in reverse, can be retraced using carbon paper or graphite paper to transfer it to the block. If the drawing is in pencil, and the drawing laid against the surface and burnished from the back, a light coating of graphite will transfer to the block. A photocopy can be made, and acetone, lacquer thinner, or other solvents can be used to lift the toner from the drawing and transfer it to the block by burnishing, leaving some time for the solvents and toner to dry. In all of these processes, the drawing must be fixed with tape to the block before burnishing. The block can be painted white for better contrast, though some solvents will dissolve paint.

Of course, the drawing can be made directly onto the block; india ink is a traditional means. The right and left sides will, of course, be reversed.

Transfer via offset

Engravers and cutters on wood and linoleum sometimes want to copy an image from one block to another, either to duplicate it or to modify it for the printing of a second color. The image can be easily copied and transferred to a second block using a printing press.

The finished block is locked up in the press and printed onto a sheet of mylar taped to the tympan. The finished block is then removed from the press, and the second block is placed in the same position. The form rollers are lifted so that the second block is not inked by them. Then the ink *from the mylar* is transferred or offset onto the second block.

Work and turn

When text or rule that runs in perpendicular directions is to be printed, it is simplest to print with two impressions, one for each direction of text or rule. The two forms needed can be placed side by side in one form and printed in a process called *work and turn*.

With the form precisely laid out, the sheet is printed with the normal material on one half of the sheet and the perpendicular material on the other half. After the first impression, the sheet is turned 180 degrees, and one form is imprinted over the other.

Skeletonizing

When text within a form is to be printed in a second color, in a separate press run, it may save time to set all of the type at once, and then *skeletonize* it. If the work is to be printed as a black text with occasional red words interspersed, for example, set the type in the usual way, and take each line that contains red words back into the stick. Remove the red type from the line, and replace it with spaces. When the spaces are placed, flip them in the stick so that part of them remains in the line, with their feet resting on the lead or slug. Then fill the next line with spaces from the left, using the protruding spaces from the line just skeletonized as a guide. Flip the skeletonized spaces back in their place, and insert the red type. Fill that line with spaces to justify the line.

Another method is to unlock the form, and hand ink the type which is to be printed in the second color. This technique was used extensively before the mid-18th century.

Creasing

Creasing or scoring is a method of crushing the paper fibers so that a clean fold can be made; the process is especially important for heavier papers, and those that fold poorly with other methods. A pamphlet cover can be creased so that the folds along the spine are precisely positioned for the block inside, or an invitation can be creased so that it is ready to fold quickly by hand. Creasing is usually done as a separate operation from printing, using a dull steel rule called a creasing rule. The rule is locked up in a press with the ink rollers removed.

Channel matrix is a thin, adhesive-backed plastic strip that mates with the face of creasing rule to form a more perfect crease. Different sizes are made for different papers and for different heights of rule. By placing the matrix directly on the rule and closing the press, the matrix is applied to the tympan in the correct position.

Blind stamping

Blind stamping is an impression made with an un-inked relief surface in paper. The process typically requires more pressure than that used for printing.

Embossing

Embossing is the three-dimensional molding of a paper surface. A male and female die is typically used, and the dies are usually heated. A great deal of pressure is required, and specially-made presses that can withstand the strain are needed. While it is certainly possible to emboss with a hand cylinder or platen press, the process isn't recommended, as a die of any size will require enough impression force to quickly wear out the press.

Embossing can be registered with existing printing, or it can be plain (or *blind*). Metallic foil is often used to give the embossing a metallic coating, frequently gold or silver.

Perforating

Perforations for tickets and forms can be made with perforating rule, though printers must be cautious about overworking their press when perforating large areas. Perforating rule is usually run on cylinder presses, though small amounts can be run on platen presses. To protect the platen or cylinder, the rule should bear against a steel backing. Most printers use strips of steel backing material with teeth that hold it in position on the tympan.

20

Lubrication

Presses will wear out quickly if not lubricated, and it will surprise many press owners to learn that manufacturers generally specified daily lubrication for at least some part of their press.

On any press, there are many lubrication points, most with an oil hole. *Every part that moves requires lubrication.* It is helpful to slowly work the press and observe, in minute detail, what parts move and where they should be lubricated. A bit of probing may be needed to investigate linkages and parts that are buried within the cabinetry or frame.

Once the machine's movements are understood, a lubrication routine should always begin at the same place on the press, and proceed around it in a regular pattern. Carry a rag when oiling, and wipe up any spilled oil from the surface of the press. A few drops is sufficient for most parts. Those parts that do more than their share of work or whose bearing surfaces are especially large, such as the side arms, the main shaft, and the rocker shaft on a platen press, can have several copious squirts. It is not possible to do damage with too much oil, though oil must be kept away from surfaces that carry ink or paper, and from electric motors and boxes.

The oil holes are useless if filled with dirt, and a small dental tool or a drill bit held in the hand should be used to clean them if necessary. It is sometimes best to remove a part from a machine to clean a thoroughly plugged oil hole. Occasionally one will find a moving part that should be lubricated but that doesn't have an oil hole. The really diligent can remove the part and drill a hole. The less diligent can drop oil onto the part where the oil will spread across the bearing surfaces.

A machine oil of 20 weight is recommended for both platen and cylinder presses. Vandercook specified 40 weight oil for form roller bearings, which the company said should be lubricated daily. If 20 weight oil isn't available, 30 weight can be used. If automotive motor oil is all that can be found, obtain a non-detergent one, which will adhere better to open surfaces. The late John Hern of Idaho, who understood machines and printing well, recommended way oil for presses, an oil designed for the ways of lathes and machine tools. "It is light," he wrote, "so will penetrate small clearances easily, and has a high-tack additive to stick to the bearings without running off."

Gears should occasionally be coated with a small amount of grease. Open parts where oil won't be contained, such as the treadle hook of a platen press, are better greased than oiled.

Electric motors should receive a drop of 20 weight oil in their oil cups or oil holes every six months. They should not be given any more oil, as it can penetrate the motor and cause electrical faults. Many older motors give lubrication instructions on their rating plates. Newer motors have sealed bearings and can't be lubricated.

Platen press lubrication

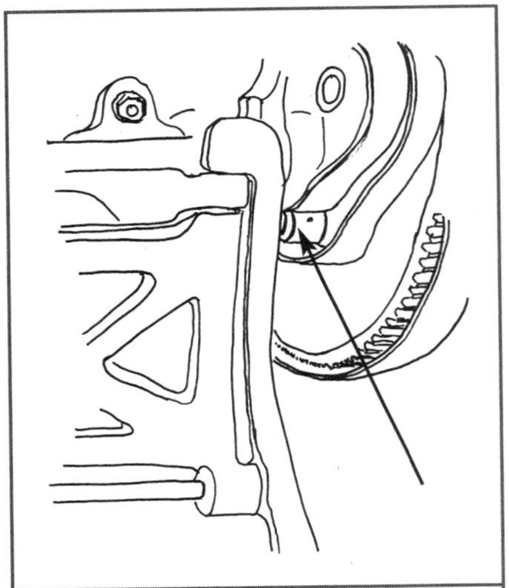

A platen press should be lubricated every time it is used, and if used continuously throughout the day, it should be lubricated every three to four hours. Most platen presses have simple bearing surfaces, with a metal shaft in direct contact with its mating surface, and these surfaces need a film of oil to prevent wear.

On a large platen press, the cam follower, which rocks the platen from feeding position to printing position, is often neglected. This small roller is buried within one of the press's *wheels,* and is difficult to find. On a C&P 10 × 15, the follower can be oiled from the front of the press or from the side. To oil from the front, the press is nearly closed and the flywheel is rotated with one hand until the oil hole in the follower rises into position to receive oil. An oil can with a spout at least 5 inches long is needed; 8 inches is better. From the side, the follower is oiled through an access hole in the large wheel. The cam follower is in position when the press is almost fully open, with the hole in the wheel just past 3 o'clock.

FIGURE 81
The cam follower on a C&P platen press is well-hidden within the wheel on the right side of the press. It is often overlooked when oiling.

Cylinder press lubrication

Most cylinder presses have a combination of sophisticated needle and ball-bearings and simple bearing surfaces. For the typical cylinder press, manufacturers recommended weekly lubrication, with the exception of the form roller bearings on Vandercooks, for which the company specified daily lubrication. For presses used more than 50 hours per week, Vandercook specified oiling every 50 hours. If the press is used occasionally, it should be lubricated every time it is used.

On a cylinder press, the bearing rails on each side of the bed should be cleaned and oiled daily, and the bearing surfaces on the cylinder should receive similar attention. On a Challenge press with a moveable bed, a pool of oil should be left on the track of the bed bearing frame; the roller bearings underneath the bed will pick up the oil as they pass.

Vandercook and Challenge both specified petroleum jelly for the shaft of the *worm vibrator* or distributor in the ink system of their cylinder presses. For the grippers, they both recommended fine machine oil, but some printers have taken to using graphite. On a cylinder press, the main bearings on which the cylinder turns are typically sealed, and are only serviced if the press is overhauled.

21

Safety

Machine tending

Around machines, printers should keep their hair tied back, and their jewelry off. Clothes should be kept tightly attached around the body, rather than loose. I discourage the wearing of aprons around machines.

Lead

(A list of the references cited below appears as an appendix.)

Lead enters the body when lead-laden dust is inhaled, and when large particles that contain lead are swallowed. These large particles may contaminate food or drink, or may enter the mouth from contact with the hands. Very little lead passes through the skin.

The body does not metabolize lead into any other form; it is stored in bone, released to the blood, and slowly excreted in urine and feces over several weeks. With continued exposure to lead, the body's ability to excrete it is soon overwhelmed.

Lead can affect almost every organ system in the body, replacing calcium, binding with many of the body's proteins, and interfering with many of the body's basic metabolic processes. Most sensitive to the effects of lead are the central nervous system and the blood; in red blood cells, lead inhibits the formation of hemoglobin. Lead also damages the kidneys, the reproductive system, the brain, and the heart.

Symptoms of lead toxicity can be subtle after long-term, low level exposure, or dramatic after a short-term, high dose exposure. Long-term occupational lead exposure in adults has resulted in anemia, weakness of the fingers, wrists and ankles, and reduced scores on nervous system function tests compared to non-exposed adults.

Studies over the past 90 years have consistently found that commercial letterpress printers have higher blood and urine lead concentrations than the general public, but the concentrations seldom reach toxic levels (1,5,6). In general, industrial hygienists have not considered the lead levels in printers' blood hazardous, and no greater risk of death or cancer among printers has been reported (1,6,7). The scientific view of safe limits has changed, however, as our understanding of the negative health effects of low-level lead exposure grows. Currently, the "advisory level of concern" for blood lead in adults set by OSHA, the Occupational Safety and Health Administration, is 40 μg/dl. The Centers for Disease Control and Prevention, or CDC, however, has set its "level of concern" for adults at 25 μg/dl, and has proposed that the U.S. reduces lead exposure so that, by 2010, no adults have blood lead levels greater than 25 μg/dl (7).

The current level of concern for blood lead in children, however, is 10 μg/dl. Recent studies suggest that there is no safe level of lead for young children, who may suffer developmental effects, including IQ loss, at levels below 10 μg/dl.

Though type is composed mostly of lead, very little lead is found in the air of print shops, even when type is being cast. In fact, there is reliable data to show that airborne lead levels in large American commercial typesetting, Linotype, and Monotype shops from the 1940s to the 1970s were well below the current OSHA standard of 50 μg/m³. Typically, measured airborne lead levels were less than 1 μg/m³ (1,2,5).

However, dust from the floor and other surfaces in print shops can be heavily contaminated with lead. Dust samples taken from the pavement just outside newspaper plants in London in 1984 (2) and from the floor of a home printery in Japan (3) were astonishingly high in lead content. The street dust near the newspaper plants ranged from 8,000 to more than 39,000 ppm (parts per million) lead, while typical street dust measured 1,360 to 3,400 ppm lead. Dust in the home printery ranged from 422 to 20,386 ppm lead, while dust in the typical home was 42 to 373 ppm lead. A 1998 study of occupational lead exposure in 90 Mexican printers found low lead concentrations in the air, but very high levels on hands before washing (4).

These studies suggest that the major risk from lead in typesetting shops is from ingestion of lead-contaminated dust particles by hand-to-mouth contact. Clearly, one should not eat, drink, or smoke in a letterpress shop, and one should never put type in the mouth. Thorough hand washing before eating is very important. Dust collected from sweeping or cleaning should be discarded, and not tossed out the door.

Children, who are more sensitive than adults to the effects of lead, also have more contact with the floor, and they place their hands in and around their mouths more frequently. They should not be allowed to play in a print shop.

A vacuum cleaner should be used to clean type cases; if compressed air is used, a dust mask should be worn, and the work should be done outside. Printers should use a "high-efficiency particulate air" (or "HEPA") vacuum cleaner to collect dust, since ordinary vacuum cleaners can suspend more fine particles into the air than they pick up. A HEPA vacuum is designed to filter particles as small as 0.3 microns, with a micron being 1 millionth of a meter, and a human hair about 100 microns in width.

Printers should wear coveralls over their clothes, or change clothes before coming home. Shoes worn in the shop should stay in the shop. Clothes worn in the shop should be washed separately from other clothes. Ideally, the printer would shower when returning home.

Finally, a shop with lead type should not be part of regular living space, where dust can travel from the shop to other rooms.

Solvents

Increasing awareness of the health effects of some solvents has led to a growing movement toward less toxic materials in print shops. Chemicals used in industry in the U.S., Canada, and many other countries are now accompanied by a Material Safety Data Sheet which shows the ingredients and the known health risks for those ingredients. MSDSs are available from manufacturers, and many are available on the internet. It is best to obtain the MSDS issued by the manufacturer of the product being used, since the components of some composition products, such as mineral spirits, will vary from one maker to the next.

Solvents used in the print shop enter the body mostly by inhalation. Absorption through the skin is limited because petroleum distillates evaporate quickly. The major signs of toxicity are respiratory tract irritation and neurologic effects (specifically, excitation followed by depression). Skin irritation can be significant after prolonged contact.

Good ventilation is essential to reduce inhalation, but good ventilation is often impossible to achieve. Suffice it so say that if you feel lightheaded, dizzy, or drowsy while using solvents, leave the area. If there are persistent symptoms, consult your healthcare provider. Goggles should be designed for chemical protection; gloves should be impermeable to the solvent you are using.

Glove manufacturers can tell you which materials resist particular chemicals. Most material safety data sheets (MSDS) show the best glove material in the section titled "Protective Equipment." Viton, Nitrile, and Neoprene are the best materials for protection against VMP naphtha and mineral spirits.

I continue to use mineral spirits as the primary solvent in my shop, but I prefer to clean presses at the end of the day, and then leave the shop.

Non-toxic solvents

The toxic effects of solvent can be reduced by using so-called non-toxic solvents, many of which use orange oil, which is found in lemons and oranges, and technically known as Limonene, d- Limonene or l-Limonene. There is an extensive literature developing on this subject, and excellent results have been reported by letterpress printers using these products. The suppliers of printmaking crafts such as stone lithography and intaglio are a good source for non-toxic solvents.

Solvents and fire

Rags containing flammable solvents may ignite through oxidation if left closely confined and compressed. "If a printer wishes to have a fire," wrote Henry Bishop in 1889, "he need only allow a pile of . . . dirty rags to lie in some corner until spontaneous combustion takes place, for which he will not have long to wait."

Use a fireproof waste can in your shop for used rags, or leave solvent-covered rags open and carefully laid-out so that the solvent evaporates safely. The danger of fire can be reduced by using non-flammable solvents.

22

Tools for the Letterpress Shop

General shop equipment

A shop should have a supply of rags, and should be equipped with a pencil sharpener, one or more fire extinguishers, a waste basket, and a fire-proof waste can.

A range of mechanic's tools should be housed in the shop, including a carpenter's hammer, a mechanic's hammer, some punches, a set of socket wrenches, a set of combination wrenches, crescent wrenches, pliers, a needle-nosed pliers, a file, a trouble light, and a half-dozen screwdrivers of different sizes. Each printer should examine his or her equipment for fittings that require special tools, such as allen or metric heads, and have these tools on hand before they are needed. A tool box makes it easy to move the tools about en masse and saves many steps.

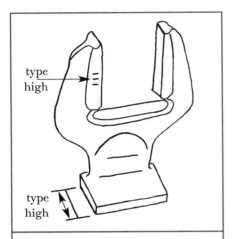

type high

type high

FIGURE 82
A type gauge.
The central of the three marks indicates the point at which the throat, which is slightly tapered, is .918 inches in width; the marks on each side of this indicate a thousandth of an inch high and a thousandth of an inch low. The base of the gauge is often designed to measure .918 inches as well.

Cabinets

Shops should have cabinets for furniture, cabinets or cases for leads and slugs, and a galley cabinet (or *rack*). An imposing surface is needed for platen press work. Some imposing stone cabinets incorporate racks for furniture, leads and slugs, and galleys.

Cabinets for type sometimes have lead and slug storage in a shelf above the cabinet, and they often have a slanted top on which a case may be placed for typesetting. Slanted iron brackets may also be fixed to a cabinet with a flat top to hold cases.

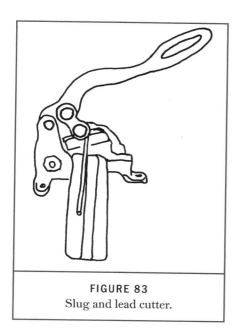

FIGURE 83
Slug and lead cutter.

Tables and benches will be needed for paper and small tools. Since printers spend most of their working time on their feet, a comfortable chair or two is important for breaks.

Rags

Rags should be lint-free and absorbent, and should be free of any metal or plastic hardware. Knits, especially cotton T-shirts, work well as rags. Cheap T-shirts can usually be bought at a church or school rummage sale.

Essential tools for the letterpress printer

Hand slug cutter Used for shortening leads and slugs. Often more convenient than a tabletop cutter.

Galleys Used for storing type, either as it is being composed, or for long periods of time. A small cabinet holds 50 galleys.

Galley magnets Strong magnets used to keep type from tumbling.

Gauge pins Small steel clips that are pinned into the tympan paper on a hand-fed platen press. The paper is fed to them, and they hold the paper on the tympan.

Glue or paste Handy for makeready.

Hell box A box or can into which damaged type is thrown.

Tape dispenser Handy for makeready, general use.

Oil can Needed for lubricating machinery. A long spout is needed for a platen press.

Pica ruler Used to measure furniture and other material.

Scissors Handy for makeready, general use.

Exacto knife Handy for makeready, general use.

Composing stick Used to assemble the type as it is picked from the cases.

Quoins, quoin key Used to lock up forms.

Tweezers Used for making corrections in forms.

Solvent can Used for washing up the press, form.

Ink knife Used for lifting ink out of the can and distributing it on the press.

Planer Used to level or plane type.

Mallet Used to strike the planer.

Pencils Used to mark proofs, etc.

Dictionary Used to determine the correct spelling of words when setting type.

Optional tools

Most printers will occasionally use the following.

Etcher's burnisher Used for smoothing down areas on a tympan disturbed by gauge pins.

Etcher's dry point needle Used for working with type.

Etcher's scraper Used to scrape down portions of rule and plates that are not meant to print.

Glass ink table Used to roll out and mix small amounts of ink. A piece of stone or metal will also serve.

Roller setting gauge Used to adjust the height of rollers on a press.

Type brush Used to clean the form.

Type high gauge Used to test the height of type and mounted plates. Both hand-held and table-top models are available.

Center finding rule Used to find the center point of a line. Makes layout fast and easy.

Miter trimmer Used to trim rule to 45 degrees for borders. Can also be used to trim rules and other material square.

Ink brayer Used for creating quick proofs, to avoid inking a press.

Magnifying loupe Used to examine type and proofs.

Funnel Used for transferring liquid from bulk containers to smaller ones.

Hammer and punch Used to knock down portions of plates, and nails in plates, that are not meant to print.

23

The Letterpress Studio or Shop

The raw space

Successful printing occurs in all kinds of environments. Some printers temporarily appropriate a space in their home or garage, removing or storing their equipment after each session. Others amass large collections of type and machinery, requiring a dedicated shop. While many fine studios have been set up in a spare bedroom or a living room, health concerns, discussed in the chapter on safety, make this a poor choice. A shop set up in a shed or garage, away from living quarters, is a better choice, especially if children are present.

The difference between a studio and a shop is the size and position of the biggest door. A *studio* has a door through which everything can be hand-carried; a *shop* has a door through which the largest piece is inserted with a forklift or rolled.

A functional printing space has good natural light, suitable flooring, adequate electrical service, and a comfortable atmosphere with regular heat and dehumidification. The cleaner the space and air, the better. Dust from any source, including farm fields and woodworking equipment, must be avoided.

Basements

Avoid making use of a basement space that has no direct doorway to the outside and thus no easy way to move equipment in and out. High humidity, poor light, and an oppressive atmosphere are common to many basement shops.

Making a plan

Before setting up a shop in a new space, draw an accurate plan of the space on graph paper. Then make scale drawings of all equipment and cabinets, cut these out, and move them around on the plan until you have a satisfactory layout.

If you are moving your shop from one place to another, the paper plan can help you to load the truck in a logical manner, so that the equipment going to the back of the shop comes off the truck first.

The basic layout

The layout for a shop is usually the result of compromises involving the light, the open space, the wiring for the machinery, and the positioning of the equipment. Once you have identified a space that you wish to make your shop or studio, begin by considering the light.

Natural and electric light

Arrange your shop so that natural light from windows, doors, and skylights falls effectively on the equipment and cabinets, and glare is kept out of printers' eyes.

Both the light and the glare should be evaluated from the standpoint of the printer, remembering that he or she will spend most of their time standing at presses and type cabinets. Position equipment so that the best light is allocated to the take-off table on a platen press, the bed of a cylinder press, the imposing surfaces, and the top of type cabinets. At the same time, keep the sources of light behind or to the side of the printer to avoid glare.

A copy of the shop's basic plan can be used to sketch "bubbles" around each of the windows and glazed doors to indicate where the light is going to fall, making the bubbles larger for the south-facing openings, which will admit more light and more glare during midday. Those of you south of the equator will, of course, make the bubbles larger for the *north*-facing windows.

If you are building or remodeling and are able to install windows, remember that windows on the side *opposite* the sun bring in the most pleasant, consistent light. Windows *high on the wall* will bring in more light and less glare than low windows. Skylights bring in the best and most diffused light, again, from the direction opposite the sun.

Position the equipment in relation to the natural light and install electric lights after the equipment is in place. Concentrated electric light or *task light* should be thrown onto surfaces where you will be working with type and reviewing printed sheets: the bed of a cylinder press, imposing surfaces, the top of type cabinets, the take-off table on a platen press, and work tables. Task light should be supplemented with general room light, which illuminates areas that would otherwise be a mix of strong light and shadow; many use fluorescent lights for this. Cable lights with 12 volt halogen bulbs provide excellent task light for small areas; spot or flood bulbs can be used to concentrate or disperse the light, respectively. Alternatively, old style hanging lights with metal shades can be positioned over your equipment.

If the electric lights in your space are already in place and you want to avoid the trouble of installing new or additional lights, then the layout for your shop will have to take their effect into account. But the task lights described above are very easy to install.

Open space

Printers need space as they work and move about, and equipment should be arranged so that one can move efficiently from one end of the shop to the other. About three feet is a reasonable width for a walkway. If you plan on sharing your space with other printers who will work concurrently, allow extra open space. If you plan to teach or give demonstrations, allow abundant open space.

Position presses so that all sides of the press can be conveniently approached for lubrication and other maintenance.

Relationship of neighboring equipment

Arrange equipment so that each piece best supports its neighbors. Small cylinder presses need furniture and tools for measuring, lock-up, and planing; an imposing stone, table, or furniture cabinet near the tail of the press will save steps. Platen presses need an imposing stone or other surface for locking up the form; place it nearby. Each press should have a neighboring work table on which to lay out paper before and after printing; one with good light makes a handy place to review proofs and printed sheets.

On the other hand, type cabinets can be kept at some distance from the presses, since typesetting and printing occur as distinct activities. Likewise paper cutters, and supplies of ink and paper stock, are used occasionally and can be placed where you will.

Electric wiring for presses

It's best to run wiring directly from the wall to a press without crossing a walkway or work area. If a press must be situated in the middle of your space, away from walls, use cord covers to shield the wire, but avoid routing the wire through heavily used areas. Cord covers are available in both vinyl and metal.

Electric power

A shop will need a moderate amount of power for lights and equipment. The ideal method of wiring a shop is with rigid metal conduit. Conduit is safe, and it's easy to modify. If you're handy, it's possible to wire your shop, or make modifications, yourself; there are many excellent books on wiring to assist you.

Motors on small presses normally run on *household current:* single phase, alternating current at 110 volts. This is the current that is typically supplied to homes and commercial buildings in the U.S., Mexico, and Canada.

If you acquire equipment designed for 220 volts, you will need either to provide the proper wiring, or replace the machine's motor with a compatible one designed for 110 volts.

The remainder of this section discusses 220 volt motors and how to supply power to them. More information on electric motors is provided in the chapter on printing presses, pages 86–88.

In a typical electrical installation, two *legs* of single phase 110 volts are included, so that a supply of current taken from both will provide *single phase* 220 volts. Homes typically use this kind of current to run clothes dryers, electric cooking ranges, heavy pumps, air conditioners, and water heaters. This 220 volt current usually runs from the distribution panel (which contains the circuit breakers or fuses) over special circuits to where it is needed. To wire your shop for machinery using 220 volts, therefore, you may have to install a new run of wire from the distribution panel to the shop.

If the machinery uses *three-phase* 220 volt current, you will probably have to install a converter as well, since three-phase current isn't generally available outside of commercial and industrial areas.

Three-phase current can be manufactured on site with mechanical or "rotary" converters that use single phase current to spin a three-phase generator. This approach is preferable to using an electronic converter, sometimes called a "static converter," because static converters don't produce true 3-phase power except when starting the motor. Once running, the motor operating on a static converter has power supplied to only two of its three windings and can produce only two-thirds of its rated horsepower. Static converters aren't really suitable for printing presses because of the prolonged starting time required and the frequent starts and stops. In addition, a static converter may not properly operate the heaters on typecasting equipment.

When trying to set up a machine that is equipped with a three-phase motor in space where three-phase current isn't available, you will have to weigh the cost and convenience of installing a rotary converter, or of changing the machine's motor to one that is compatible with your available current. A converter must be oversized, or rated for more horsepower than the motor, in order to properly start it.

Plumbing

If possible, install a sink in your shop for hand washing. I have often worked without one, however, by using a washbowl and carrying buckets of water to the shop. When it's time to refresh the water, I toss the waste water on the ground outside.

Flooring

Printers spend hours on their feet tending presses or setting type, and some kind of cushioning for the feet and legs is almost a necessity. Wood, composition, or carpet are all hugely superior to concrete. Some printers prefer carpet because it's easy on type that is accidentally dropped to the floor. But carpet soon gets grungy around presses from oil and spilled ink.

A floor must be strong enough to support the weight of the type and presses. With a floor built on wood joists, the weight of equipment can be distributed across several joists by using planks or beams above the floor, and the floor can be considerably strengthened with one or more posts set beneath the joists.

To set posts, use adjustable steel posts made for supporting or leveling floors. The pressure of the post should be distributed by a cross beam at the top of the posts which spans several joists. If the bottom of the joists aren't level, use wood shims to fill gaps between the beam and joists. At the bottom, the post should rest on a pad of wood of moderate size. Posts set directly on a concrete floor can crack it.

A platen press or powered cylinder press generates a fair amount of vibration which is transferred through a wood-joist floor to surrounding spaces, including those above and below. When I had my shop in a commercial storefront in a small Minnesota town, my neighbor was a watchmaker who found the motion of my platen press ill-adapted to his craft. I was able to reduce the vibration to an acceptable level by placing four posts and a pair of beams beneath the press.

If in doubt about your floor, consult a builder or architect for advice.

Access

Leave an easy access to the shop for bringing in and removing equipment. More than once, I have seen machinery abandoned in shops where presses had been lowered into basements, or placed in a space that was later walled off.

Avoid the radical disassembling of presses and other equipment; too often, the equipment suffers. Concentrate instead on finding a shop with proper access, or on creating better access to your existing shop.

Security

Any shop is tempting to thieves, who are hoping for tools that can be quickly sold. Consider an alarm for your shop which will protect it against theft, vandalism, and fire. Make sure that doors and windows are secure. Consider covering windows with panels that can be secured from the inside.

Good housekeeping will help avoid fire. Use solvents with low flammability, and dispose of solvent-laden rags in a fire-safe can or leave them open to dry. Install a fire extinguisher. Do not smoke in the shop.

Guests

When inexperienced visitors come to your shop, they should be asked to observe four rules:

1. Slide cases out only half way, to avoid dropping them from the cabinet.
2. Mind the protocol for clean and dirty surfaces, discussed below in the section on "shelves and tables."

3. Lay nothing on top of standing type.
4. Handle assembled type only with supervision.

Pests

Mice are sure to make your shop a home; the many small compartments in your typecases are just too tempting. Traps should be set from the outset; four or five of them are not too many. Cats will also help. Some printers place mothballs in their type cases to discourage mice.

Humidity control

A dehumidifier will help to control moisture in the air and prevent equipment from rusting in the summer. Air conditioners also have a dehumidifying effect. In the fall, winter, and spring, a heater or furnace will keep everything dry. The heating or dehumidifying equipment must be run continuously, though temperatures may be kept at a low level.

Shelves and tables

Plan to install small shelves for such things as ink and boxes of envelopes, and a more serious set for holding paper. Large sheets of paper will require heavy, free-standing shelves or cabinets.

Tables in a shop should be designated as "dirty" or "clean." Clean surfaces are reserved for paper and a few "clean" tools such as rulers, scissors, and small paper cutters. Type, plates, furniture, oil cans, machine parts, and ink are kept only on the dirty surfaces.

Often, white paint or a natural wood finish is used to indicate a clean surface, and dark paints are used to indicate a dirty one. The bare steel surface on the bed of a paper cutter is clean, but the bare steel surface of an imposing table is dirty. It is always wise to review this with any untrained workers who come to your shop.

All tables must be sturdy, as any one of them may be pressed into service to hold a shipment of paper, for example. A dirty surface should never be directly above a clean one.

It is surprising how much surface area the average printer will cover with ink cans, solvent, furniture, type, paper, proofs, oil cans, cutters, wrenches, planers, and rags.

24

Moving Printing Equipment

It's easy to move type and small presses that can simply be lifted and carried. To move heavier machinery, you will need planning and equipment but not much physical strength; equipment for moving, which is easily rented, will do nearly all of the work.

Professional machine movers can be hired to move machinery, and some specialize in letterpress equipment. But many printers find movers' fees exorbitant, and choose to do the work themselves. Others have hired movers only to find them relatively inexperienced. I have heard an alarming number of accounts in which "professional movers" damaged or destroyed presses or typecasters.

Moving type and type cabinets

When type is in cases which are, in turn, in a cabinet, the cases can be taken individually from the cabinet and stacked in some convenient place, preferably on a dolly. Then the empty cabinet can be moved into the truck or trailer, and the cases can be put back into the cabinet for the journey. Place type cabinets so the cases open toward the back of the truck or trailer, since the most radical force will be generated from stopping, and the cases should be forced into, rather than out of, their cabinet.

If the journey is a long one, secure the cases with a rope lashed vertically around the cabinet.

An alternative method is to move the cases separately from the cabinets. Have corrugated cardboard cut to fit as covers for the cases, and then wrap the cover and the case with plastic stretch film. The stretch film will also serve to bind together several cases, or a stack of cases.

It is helpful to mark the cases in some way so they can be returned to their proper places in the cabinet.

A pair of empty type cases can be carried in each hand, with the bottom of one against the bottom of another.

Type on galleys can be encapsulated with stretch film, and the galleys can be stacked upon themselves, within reason, by layering corrugated cardboard between them. Galleys can also be placed into cabinets in the same manner described above for type cases, but be certain to place the galleys with one of the three retaining lips toward the front of the truck, or type will walk off the galleys.

Reglet, lead, and furniture cabinets can usually be wrapped with stretch film and moved with their contents intact. Whenever leads and slugs are boxed, the boxes must be kept small.

General safety when moving

Be careful, when moving equipment, to keep people clear of equipment that may slide or fall. Before starting, explain to your help that there is no hope of arresting a wayward machine with human strength, and make it clear that you do not want them to attempt to stop a machine over which you have lost control. Hydraulic systems in jacks and forklifts can fail suddenly, and operators can make mistakes, so instruct your help never to place any part of themselves between a lift and the ground. Steel-toed boots make all moving safer.

Most disasters involve equipment that topples from steep, high ramps. Regrettably, a cast-iron machine that falls from any height usually shatters.

General supplies for moving

Nearly all supplies are available from rental shops, including moving blankets, chain, straps, casters, machine dollies, Johnson bars, trucks with tailgate lifts, and even forklifts. The rental shop staff will help you to select the right equipment and show you how to work it. To save time on moving day, I like to be briefed when making reservations, rather than on the day of the move.

Know the dimensions and the approximate weight of the machinery you plan to move when you contact the rental shop. When measuring machinery, it's helpful to note both the dimensions of the base and the overall size, including the vertical and horizontal position of anything projecting, such as feed tables, motors and drive shafts; a quick sketch is ideal. The weight of many presses is shown in the section on presses; the typical weight of a few presses and other equipment is shown below:

Estimated weight (pounds)	
Pilot platen	200
Pearl platen	800
C&P platen 8 × 12	1,050
C&P platen 10 × 15	1,500
C&P platen 12 × 18	2,100
Challenge 15 × 26 cylinder	1,000
Challenge 20 × 26 cylinder	1,400
Vandercook 4 cylinder	1,100
Vandercook SP20 cylinder	1,440
Vandercook 219 cylinder	2,300
26″ guillotine paper cutter	1,000

With any machinery move, it's important to have wooden blocks along to set machinery on temporarily, and to brace or block things during transport. Include short and long pieces of ¾ inch stock, 2 × 4s, and 4 × 4s. It is rare to have too many blocks. For large pieces of equipment, large blocks, say 8 × 8 × 24 inches or wider, will be useful. Boat yards may lend you some of their blocks.

A small dolly or furniture-type mover—a simple wood frame with casters —is a big help when moving type, cabinets, and small equipment. It's best to have several along, especially when type and cabinets are being moved. A dolly can be purchased cheaply and is handy to have around the shop. A platform truck or a hand truck may also be useful for moving.

I always bring a few empty cardboard boxes along for any move, ready for the unanticipated acquisition of spacing material, supplies, or small tools. For metal spacing material and type, keep the boxes small, or they will weigh too much to lift when only partly filled.

Equip yourself with lots of tools; the variety needed will surprise you. You may need to work on the machinery (removing parts to make the equipment lighter or smaller), on parts of the building (removing doors to make room), on the truck or trailer, and on the machinery or equipment you bring along for the move.

For any move, the following are essential things to have along:
- work gloves
- work clothes that can be sullied with dirt and grease
- tools, including an oil can
- tape measure

- machinery (or rigger's) casters, or a machine dolly, or rollers, or a pallet jack
- jacks, or a Johnson bar, or some kind of lifting equipment
- heavy straps or chain for moving and securing the load
- rope
- moving blankets
- blocks
- small dollies or platform trucks
- rags
- hand cleaner (diaper wipes work well)
- tire gauge
- heavy broom and dustpan
- plenty of help

Check tire pressure on trailers and trucks before setting out on moving day.

The following are optional:
- knee pads
- cardboard cut to galley and/or case size
- plastic wrap
- hammer and nails, 2 × 4s, crowbar
- tarps
- air compressor and blowgun at home

This list is repeated in the back of the book for quick reference on moving day.

Letterpress machinery isn't meant to get wet, so try to move in clear weather. If a move must occur in poor weather, bring some tarps along, and cover bare metal surfaces with grease, oil, or a spray. Commercial rust preventers are available in small spray cans; a silicon spray such as WD-40 will also work. Silicon sprays attract dirt, however, and should be removed with a solvent after the move.

Moving heavy machinery

The mechanics of moving are simple: the mover must lift the equipment high enough to get rollers or casters beneath it, move it across the floor to a door, lift it or roll it onto a truck, and secure it for travel. At the receiving end, the steps are reversed.

It's sometimes helpful to remove parts to make equipment more compact. On a platen press, the feedboard, the ink disk, and sometimes the flywheel or the flywheel and main shaft can be removed. On a Pearl platen press, removing the flywheel alone makes the press considerably less top-heavy. On a 10 × 15 C&P platen press, removing the flywheel with a gear-puller, pulling the main shaft, and removing the throw-off linkage reduces the width from 44 to 31 inches. On a hand cylinder press, removing the feedboard can make the press two feet shorter.

When moving a hand cylinder press, secure the cylinder with lashing or large wooden wedges to prevent it (or the bed) from moving. On a hand press, secure or remove the bed.

When moving a C&P Pilot, close the press and lash it closed with rope or wire. This press is liable to snap shut if lifted by the side arms, pinching the hand between the side arm and the arm that actuates the rollers.

The Heidelberg Windmill can be fitted with a lifting eye or a shaft placed through the base; the process is described in the chapter on presses.

Lifting machinery from the floor

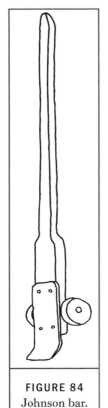

One of the most useful tools for a machinery move is a Johnson bar, a long wood or metal lever on casters with a steel flange on the working end. They are made in various lengths, and are often the first and only tool needed to lift a piece of equipment. They are extremely powerful; my wife and I once used a seven foot long Johnson bar to lift the corners of a 4,000-pound cylinder press and place casters beneath it. Many machines with pedestal bases have a small opening where the base meets the floor that will accommodate the flange of a Johnson bar. Johnson bars are sometimes called "lever dollies."

Simple bottle or mechanical jacks can also be used to lift machinery. Pallet jacks, which are manually-operated forks designed to lift wood pallets and their loads and roll them across a floor, are often sufficient to move presses, or to lift them sufficiently to set casters. They're common in small plants of all kinds, and may be available for loan from a friendly business. They require about three inches of vertical clearance and can lift two or three tons to about seven inches. A high-lifting pallet jack can lift a ton to about 30 inches. Pallet jacks weigh about 200 to 250 pounds, and cannot themselves be easily lifted.

The motion involved in lifting should be smooth and balanced, and a ma-

FIGURE 84
Johnson bar.

chine should remain as level as possible when lifted. Some equipment is top-heavy and will easily topple. Care should be taken to lift a machine so that its frame twists as little as possible. An adjustment to the machine may be required after a move to reestablish settings of rollers, the platen, or the cylinder.

Never lift equipment by bearing against a shaft, as shafts can easily be bent. Always lift the frame. On machines with sheet-metal cabinets, wood blocks or shims should be used to distribute the stress over a wide area.

Rolling machinery across a floor

Printing equipment can be moved about on pallet jacks, rollers, casters, and dollies. Usually two people can push a heavy machine.

Rollers can be made from heavy wood dowels, or plastic or steel pipe; rollers of large diameter, say three inches or more, will work much better than slight ones. The equipment to be moved should be secured to heavy pallets or wood rails; the rails should be large enough to keep the press from twisting as it is lifted and rolled. Rails of 4 × 4 inch lumber are suitable for small to medium sized platen and cylinder presses; larger ones are required for larger presses. The equipment should be attached to the pallets or rails with lag screws, wood cleats, or even bent nails. When rolling equipment, several people should be assigned to moving the rollers from the back of the machine to the front. Ideally, four people are available: two dedicated to picking up the rollers as the machine rolls away from them, and two dedicated to placing them in its path. The pick-up crew can slide the rollers across the floor to the placing crew. If equipment must be rolled over grass or gravel, rather than a smooth surface, then planks or plywood must be used under the rollers, or pneumatic casters must be used.

Rigger's or machine casters are much easier to use than rollers. They incorporate several small, heavy rollers in a steel frame. Once positioned beneath a machine, they remain in place while the machine is moved across the floor. Some have pivots and steering handles so the machine can be turned more easily. They are sometimes called "machinery skates."

Recently, a two-wheeled dolly has been introduced that straps to equipment and lifts it with small tines and an integrated hydraulic jack. Used in pairs, their large casters permit small, heavy machines to be easily rolled. Because the lifting and the rolling is handled by one piece of equipment, they simplify things. Two brand names are "Roll-a-lift" and "Rais-n-Roll."

Loading machinery onto a truck or trailer

Small presses with rollers or casters can be pushed up shallow ramps into a trailer or truck. With the help of three or four others, I have pushed both a 20×26 Challenge proof press and a 10×15 C&P platen press up a ramp. But avoid high or steep ramps, on which it is easy to loose control over the load, and avoid using a ramp for top-heavy equipment.

A chain or cable winch can be useful for pulling or stabilizing equipment, but they are slow. With a little practice, they can be used to ease equipment down a ramp as well as up.

Sometimes a small crane, such as an engine hoist, can be used to lift small equipment onto a trailer. The equipment can be suspended in the air while the trailer is rolled beneath it.

A loading dock, conventionally four feet in height, makes a truck bed level with a building's floor and eliminates the need to lift equipment into a vehicle. Docks are usually equipped with steel plates to provide a smooth transition from the truck bed to the floor, and to help as the load is moved and the truck bed rises and falls. The height of some docks can be adjusted slightly.

Lift gates are hydraulically powered platforms attached to the rear end of a truck that can raise and lower about a ton from the ground to the truck bed. But they possess two serious disadvantages for moving machinery. First, the lift platform is normally a few inches thick with a steep, beveled edge on the outside, so it's necessary to lift and roll the machinery onto the platform using ramps, jacks, or other equipment. The process is time consuming. Second, the lift platform doesn't remain level while it rises and falls, making it dangerous to lift top-heavy machines.

A forklift is the safest and speediest way to move heavy equipment onto and off of trailers or trucks. Forklifts can keep a load level, regardless of the terrain, and once positioned to lift a machine, they do all of the work—assistants can stand clear as the load is lifted and moved.

Forklifts quickly traverse any space between the shop floor and the truck. Where the terrain around a shop is sloped, one can park the truck on level ground, so moving the equipment within the truck will be easier and safer. By using beams to push and chains to pull, they can speedily position machinery within trucks.

Forklifts are often available from lumberyards, which can supply them with an operator for about $100 per session. When I purchased a medium-sized etching press in New York, the seller laid the machine horizontally on a pallet and loaded both into my suv with a forklift. When I arrived home in Minnesota, the local lumberyard sent a "piggyback" rig—a flatbed truck with a forklift that rides on the back—to unload it. The charge from the lumberyard, including operator, was about $35.

Unless you are experienced with lifting machines, hire the forklift and operator together. The operator's experience and skill will pay for itself.

Forklift capacities are rated in pounds, often with the center of the load 24 inches from the forklift end of the fork. The forks can usually be adjusted to various widths, and long forks are available for situations where roofs or other obstructions prevent the forklift from getting close to the load. Forklift tires are either pneumatic (for rough ground) or solid (for concrete floors). Because forklifts carry a considerable amount of weight to counterbalance the load, they're unusually heavy; a big one weighs 12,000 pounds.

If the ground is soft where the forklift must travel, lay down large pieces of thick plywood to support the machine and its load. Do this at the first suspicion that the ground might yield, before you discover it empirically by bogging down the forklift, or by sinking one side and upsetting the load. Planks can be used for support where the path is straight.

Trucking and trailering printing equipment

Before arriving at the pick-up site, check the tire pressure on all trucks and trailers. Tires which are under-inflated may appear normal until equipment is loaded.

Before loading, inspect equipment carefully for parts that may be caught by the wind and torn free, or loose parts that may shake free. When I moved a large cylinder press from northern Minnesota on an open trailer in 2002, I nearly lost part of the wooden feedboard that wasn't as well-attached as I had thought.

When trailering a heavy load, it must be placed with the majority of the weight on the front half of the trailer, or the trailer will wander from side to side, sometimes violently. Larger trailers designed for loads of more than a ton have their own braking systems, some of which respond to forward pressure on the tongue, and some of which use an electrical signal from the towing vehicle. Note that the coupler on the tongue of a trailer must fit the ball on the vehicle, commonly 1⅞, 2, 2¼, or 2⁵⁄₁₆ inches. The larger sizes are designed for heavier loads. Trailer lighting terminals vary as well; adapters are available for some. Cross the safety chains in an 'x' before attaching them to the vehicle.

Once equipment is loaded on a truck or trailer, secure the load well with heavy straps or chain. I once lost an empty metal type cabinet out of the back of a pickup truck when a gust of wind caught it and lifted it out of the bed. It was the last load I didn't tie down. I learned that gravity alone won't hold a heavy object in place, and that the significance of gravity decreases with speed. Now, when I hear someone say that a machine does not need to be secured because it is heavy, I remind them that a Boeing 747 weighs 350 tons, and it flies!

Four independent straps, one on each corner, are required for each medium or large piece of equipment. With four anchoring lines, one can fail and three will remain to hold the machine in place. Most of the force that must be countered will be forward when stopping, and sideways when turning.

It's important to secure machinery even when using an enclosed truck, since the walls of the average truck are only designed to keep the weather out and contain the lightest of cargo. Commercial truckers in the U.S. are required to use anchoring lines with an individual strength equal to one half the weight of the object being secured.

With chain, use *binders* to tighten the chain against the load. Two kinds of hooks are used: chain hooks, which are designed to grip a link of chain, and open hooks, which are wide enough to slide along the links. Chain hooks are usually used. Hooks should never be inserted *into* the center of the link, where they will jam, rather, they should enclose the entire link. Additional security is gained by wrapping wire around the hooks and chain where it might shake loose. This is usually unnecessary with chain binders, which cinch the chain so tightly that it's unlikely to work loose.

Straps, which are easier on the equipment and much faster to set up, usually come with an integral ratchet for tightening. If you supply your own straps, see that they mate with the rails in the truck before moving day.

If the bed of a truck or trailer is wood, a 2 × 4 can be nailed down at the base of the equipment to prevent it from sliding. Such a stop is used in addition to anchoring lines. Removal will be simplified if the nails in the stop are not driven down flush, or if duplex or double-headed nails are used.

Check your load frequently while on the road, beginning with a stop after the first three to five miles. Trucks with heavy loads will require more stopping distance and should be driven with care. Check all the lights and blinkers, especially on trailers, before setting out on each leg of the journey.

Whenever a truck or trailer is backed up, the driver should roll the windows of the truck down, and position an assistant at each rear corner. The assistants should remain in sight of the driver via the mirrors; each is responsible for their respective side and rear corner, from the ground to the top of the truck. By bringing their arms together above their heads as a truck is backing, assistants can show the driver how far the back of the truck is from the desired stopping point.

Cleaning equipment

A heavy broom or two will be useful for sweeping the path clear when rolling equipment, for cleaning floors before placing equipment, and for sweeping the truck after the move.

When you arrive home, an air compressor with a blow gun attached will make quick work of cleaning dust and dirt out of presses, cabinets, cases, and racks before bringing them inside.

Installing machinery

Whenever a floor-model press is installed, it should be leveled on both axes using a spirit level and wood shims which are driven beneath the feet. All four feet should be bearing the weight of the press; a press which rocks during the printing cycle may perform poorly.

25

Restoring & Maintaining Printing Presses

General techniques

When working on machinery, a few general principles will help to get the machine back together properly.

As you disassemble, take lots of pictures. Use a system to mimic the position of parts that are removed so they assume the same orientation that they had when attached to the machine; four bolts of varying sizes, for example, should be laid out with the bolts which were to the right *on the right,* and bolts that were *above* others placed behind those that were below. With all machinery, the heads, threads and lengths of bolts and screws may vary in subtle ways, and it's important to keep things sorted, so they're put back in the same place on the machine. If parts are removed for more than a short time, the bolts or screws should be placed back into the threaded holes that they came from for safekeeping. If lots of disassembly is done, bags or boxes can be used to isolate the parts and fasteners, and tape marked with a pen can be placed around parts to identify them.

It's often helpful to mark parts with orientations such as "left," "up," or "in" with grease pencil, a crayon, a paint stick, or some chalk. If parts are removed permanently or for a lengthy period of time, they can be tied to the machine directly with wire, or placed in a sock or cloth bag that is tied to the machine.

When replacing screws and bolts, clean threads with a wire brush and coat them with oil. Avoid replacing fasteners with modern substitutes.

Use patience and care when working on machinery. Cast iron is easily broken, and it's difficult to repair. Avoid striking machine parts directly with a hammer; use a block of wood to cushion the blow. Pull pulleys and flywheels off of shafts with a gear puller. Be willing to stop because your tools or knowledge don't fit the job.

Rust

Rust is corrosion that occurs when iron and oxygen combine to form iron oxide; the corrosion process accelerates markedly whenever water is available.

To prevent rust, the shop space should be well-enclosed with a minimum of air exchange between the inside and outside, and the air in the shop should be kept as dry as possible with air conditioning, heating, and dehumidifying equipment. The air should also be kept free of contaminants, including dust and corrosive vapors, such as acid fumes.

Automobile paste wax or specialized rust preventers will discourage rust by keeping air, dirt, and water away from a metal surface. They should be applied with a rag several times a year. Many commercial products are available from hardware, woodworking, machine, and even gun stores. Cream waxes, which contain water, should not be used on bare metal.

Once rust forms, it can be removed with an abrasive. Soak the surface with a lubricant, and grind away the rust by hand; the lubricant will float metal particles away from the surface as you work. A good combination is kerosene and sandpaper or emery cloth. Begin with a coarse grit such as 80, and progress to 100, 120, 150, and 220. A circular motion while grinding works best. If a large, flat surface is being restored, an electric sander can be used. Wear gloves when handling kerosene.

Chemical methods of rust removal are also available. Phosphoric acid is probably the best, and can be purchased as a thick fluid called *naval jelly* which is easy to handle. If rust is severe, sandblasting can be used.

Once the rust is removed, the surface can be polished with oil and steel wool or emery cloth. The surface should then be cleaned with rags and solvent, and covered with wax or rust preventer.

If you plan to store equipment for a long period of time, a rust preventing spray will quickly cover the bare metal. Some lubricants are marketed as both lubricants and rust preventers, but the best results will be had from a specialized rust preventer.

26

Copyright

Copyright laws protect artists and authors by prohibiting the duplication of their work without permission. Because printing is duplication, a printer should understand when the work of others can legitimately be reproduced. Printers should also know how to protect their own work. At a minimum, a printer should know what copyright is, how long it endures, what can and can't be protected, and when it is permissible to reproduce parts of a work that *are* protected. In addition, printers in the U.S. should be aware of the "mandatory deposit" provision in the law, which requires a publisher to deposit, in the Library of Congress, two copies of all works that are under copyright protection.

If you are planning a significant publication project, and have questions either about your right to incorporate the work of others or your ability to protect what you publish, consult an attorney familiar with copyright law.

At present, the fee to register a copyright in the U.S. is $30.

An excellent source of information is the U.S. Government's web site, "www.copyright.gov."

27

The Wayzgoose

The ancient custom of the wayzgoose is still celebrated among letterpress printers, though it often takes the form of a convention or flea market rather than a feast. The wayzgoose was first documented by Joseph Moxon in the second volume of his *Mechanick Exercises on the Whole Art of Printing,* published in 1683–4. There is speculation that a goose was traditionally served at the feast; the 'z' became part of the word *wayzgoose* after Moxon's time. Moxon wrote:

> It is also customary for all the Journey-men to make every Year new Paper Windows, whether the old will serve again or no; Because that day they make them, the Master Printer gives them a *Way-goose;* that is, he makes them a good Feast, and not only entertains them at his own House, but besides, gives them Money to spend at the Ale-house or Tavern at Night; And to this Feast, they invite the *Correcter, Founder, Smith, Joyner,* and *Inck-maker,* who all of them severally (except the *Correcter* in his own Civility) open their Purse-strings and add their Benevolence (which Workmen account their duty, because they generally chuse these Workmen) to the Master Printers: But from the *Correcter* they expect nothing, because the Master Printer chusing him, the Workmen can do him no kindness.
>
> These *Way-gooses,* are always kept about *Bartholomew-tide.* And till the Master-Printer have given this *Way-goose,* the Journey-men do not use to Work by Candle Light.

Wayzgooses are traditionally celebrated on or about the 24th of August. Herbert Davis and Harry Carter, who edited the 1958 Oxford University Press edition of Moxon, concluded that paper was likely installed in print shop windows to screen the sun, and prevent it from drying dampened paper during printing. But the notes to an edition of Moxon published by the New York Typothetae in 1896 asserts that "windows of glass were unusual."

The "civility" mentioned in reference to the corrector seems to refer to a gratuity.

APPENDIX I

Sources used in the section on presses

Information on presses was taken from a variety of manufacturers' catalogues and advertisements, as well as from a number of articles and books. Much information was taken from the following:

Eckmann, James. *Heritage of the Printer.* Philadelphia: North American Publishing, 1965. Green, Ralph. *A History of the Platen Jobber.* Chicago: Printing Office of P. Reed, 1953. Harris, Elizabeth M. *Printing Presses in the Graphic Arts Collection: Printing, Embossing, Stamping and Duplicating Devices.* Washington, D.C.: National Museum of American History, Smithsonian Institution, 1996. Harrison, John. "Platen Press Buyers' Guide." *Type & Press,* Winter, 1983. Hoch, Fred W. *Handbook for Pressmen.* New York: Fred W. Hoch Associates, 1943. Moran, James. *Printing Presses: History and Development from the Fifteenth Century to Modern Times.* Berkeley, Calif.: University of California Press, 1973. Sterne, Harold E. "History of Vandercook." *Letterpress Green Sheet,* Ada, Mich., March, 2004, Issue 6. Sterne, Harold E. *Catalogue of Nineteenth Century Printing Presses.* Cincinnati: Ye Old Printery, 1978. Sterne, Harold E. "Short History of Vandercook." Manuscript provided by the author. Williams, Fred. "The Great Colt's Armory War!" *Type & Press,* Winter, 1983. Williams, Fred. "The Miehle Vertical" *Type & Press,* Summer, 1982. Williams, Fred. "The Official Press." *Type & Press,* Spring, 1982. Williams, Fred. "Original Heidelberg, 'the Prince of Presses.'" *Type & Press,* Summer, 1981. Williams, Fred. "The Pilot: a Splendid Little Press." *Type and Press,* Winter, 1984. Williams, Fred. "Sigwalt: Too Good a Press to Let Die?" *Type and Press,* Summer, 1979. Williams, Fred. "The Rise and Fall of the Kelly Press." *Type & Press,* Spring, 1985. Williams, Fred. "Vandy: A Splendid Press!" *Type & Press,* Winter, 1991.

References cited in the section on lead in the "Safety" chapter

1. David Michaels, Stephen R. Zoloth, et al., "Does Low-Level Lead Exposure Increase Risk of Death? A Mortality Study of Newspaper Printers." *International Journal of Epidemiology,* vol. 20, no. 4, 1991: pp. 978–983.

2. Robert A. Jensen, and Duncan P.H. Laxen, "Sources of Lead in Urban Dust: Identification of a Contribution from Newspaper Printworks." *The Science of the Total Environment,* 46, 1985: pp. 19–27.

3. M. Kawai, H. Toriumi, et al., "Home Lead-Work as a Potential Source of Lead Exposure for Children." *International Archives of Occupational and Environmental Health,* v. 53, 1983: pp. 37–46.

4. Guadalupe Aguilar-Madrid, Gregory M. Piacitelli, et al., "Exposición Ocupacional a Plomo Inorgánico en una Imprenta de la Ciudad de México." *Salud Pública de México*, vol. 41, no. 1, Enero–Febrero 1999: pp. 42–54.

5. Harold W. Ruf, and Elston L. Belknap, "Studies on the Lead Hazards in Certain Phases of Printing: I. Actual Lead Exposures as Measured by the Amount of Lead in Printing Atmospheres; II. Actual Lead Absorption as Measured by Physical Examinations, Blood and Urine Studies." *Journal of Industrial Hygiene and Toxicology,* vol. 22, no. 10, Dec. 1940: pp. 445–471.

6. Petter Kristensen and Aage Andersen, "A Cohort Study on Cancer Incidence in Offspring of Male Printing Workers." *Epidemiology,* vol. 3, no. 1, January, 1992: pp. 6–10.

7. Center for Disease Control and Prevention, "Adult Blood Lead Epidemiology and Surveillance—United States, 2002." *Morbidity and Mortality Weekly Report,* vol. 53, no. 26, July 9, 2002: pp. 578–582.

APPENDIX II

Chandler and Price dates of manufacture

Using the serial number, the year of manufacture for the common models of Chandler and Price platen presses can be derived from the list below. The serial number is stamped into the upper left corner of the bed.

Old Series Presses

8 x 12		10 x 15	
25001 to 25052	1887	302 to 501	1884
25053 to 25378	1888	502 to 555	1885
25379 to 25810	1889	556 to 857	1886
25811 to 26364	1890	858 to 1137	1887
26365 to 26891	1891	1138 to 1455	1888
26891 to 27520	1892	1456 to 1833	1889
27521 to 27988	1893	1834 to 2335	1890
27989 to 28710	1894	2336 to 2901	1891
28711 to 29700	1895	2902 to 3567	1892
29701 to 30555	1896	3568 to 4047	1893
30555 to 31626	1897	4048 to 4822	1894
31627 to 32900	1898	4822 to 5841	1895
32901 to 34206	1899	5842 to 6701	1896
34207 to 35632	1900	6702 to 7901	1897
35633 to 37038	1901	7602 to 8655	1898
37039 to 39400	1902	8656 to 9907	1899
39401 to 41040	1903	9908 to 11131	1900
41041 to 42888	1904	11132 to 12297	1901
42889 to —	1905	12298 to 14999	1902
B1 to B518	1905	14100 to 15839	1903
B519 to B1725	1906	15840 to 17675	1904
B1726 to B2907	1907	17676 to —	1905
B2908 to B3650	1908	C1 to —	1905
B3651 to B4700	1909	C601 to —	1906
B4701 to B5526	1910	C1801 to —	1907
B5527 to —	1911	C3201 to —	1908

Old Series Presses	
10 x 15 continued	
C4001 to 6473	1909
C6474 to 7420	1910
C7421 to 7575	1912
C7576 to —	1913
12 x 18	
22001 to 22021	1892
22022 to 22067	1893
22068 to 22075	1894
22176 to 22302	1895
22303 to 22457	1896
22458 to 22669	1897
22670 to 22900	1898
22901 to 23135	1899
23136 to 23353	1900
23354 to 233621	1901
23622 to 23950	1902
23951 to 23269	1903
24270 to 24604	1904
24605 to —	1905
D1 to D313	1905
D314 to D761	1906
D762 to D1312	1907
D1313 to D1628	1908
D1629 to D2251	1909
D2252 to D2801	1910
D2802 to D3222	1911
D3223 to D3224	1912
D3351 to —	1913

New Series Presses	
8 x 12	
B50000 to B50200	1912
B50201 to B51005	1913
B51006 to B51676	1914
B51677 to B52377	1915
B52378 to B58950	1916–1925
B58951 to B61502	1926–1930
B61503 to B62300	1931–1935
B62301 to B62850	1936–1940
B62851 to B63077	1941–1945
B63078 to B64159	1946–1950
B64160 to B64565	1951–1955
B64566 to B64751	1956–1960
B64752 to B64780	1961–1962
10 x 15	
XC100 to XC102	1925–1927
XC103 to XC163	1931–1933
XC164 to XC202	1934–1936
XC203 to XC236	1937–1941
10 x 15	
C50,100 to C53,671	1911–1915
C53,672 to C67,101	1916–1925
C67,102 to C71,300	1926–1930
C71,301 to C71,987	1931–1935
C71,988 to C72,667	1936–1940
C72,668 to C72,901	1941–1946
C72,902 to C76,100	1947–1950
C76,101 to C76,666	1951–1955
C76,667 to C77,077	1956–1960
C77,078 to C77,168	1961–1965
12 x 18	
X100 to X2101	1921–1925
X2102 to X3548	1926–1930
X3549 to X3794	1931–1935
X3795 to X3846	1936–1941

APPENDIX III

Vandercook date of manufacture

With a few exceptions noted in the separate table below (for models 0, 01, etc.), Vandercook numbered presses consecutively without regard to model. From September 30, 1909, when the company was started, until June 1914, Vandercook manufactured about 280 presses without serial numbers. On June 23, 1914 they shipped a model 17 with serial number 1. Below is the serial number of the first press manufactured each year.

Serial numbers on Vandercook presses are usually found on the tail of the bed, or on a plate mounted on the cabinet.

Year	Serial	Year	Serial	Year	Serial
1915	56	1938	7,649	1961	21,016
1916	124	1939	8,100	1962	21,629
1917	332	1940	8,613	1963	22,635
1918	569	1941	9,110	1964	23,425
1919	652	1942	9,700	1965	24,630
1920	1,397	1943	9,765	1966	25,603
1921	1,472	1944	9,854	1967	26,475
1922	1,533	1945	9,893	1968	27,255
1923	1,649	1946	9,912	1969	28,195
1924	1,838	1947	10,333	1970	28,727
1925	2,135	1948	12,146	1971	29,093
1926	2,492	1949	13,306	1972	29,145
1927	2,926	1950	13,947	1973	29,652
1928	3,446	1951	14,802	1974	29,807
1929	4,103	1952	15,477	1975	29,931
1930	4,895	1953	15,950	1976	30,004
1931	5,456	1954	16,549	1984	30,126
1932	5,755	1955	17,404		
1933	5,814	1956	18,040		
1934	6,024	1957	18,419		
1935	6,180	1958	18,957		
1936	6,491	1959	19,489		
1937	7,047	1960	20,123		

Rebuilt presses	
1958	50,000
1959	50,011
1960	50,021
1961	50,037
1962	50,049
1963	50,059
1964	50,068
1965	50,080
1966	50,097
1967	50,107
1968	50,142

Models 0, 01, 03 & 099
had different serial numbers.

1929	0101
1930	0206
1931	01248
1932	01629
1933	01837
1934	02390
1935	02958
1936	03359
1937	03934
1938	04526
1939	04930
1940	05318
1941	05725
1942	06183
1944	06322
1945	06345
1946	06351
1947	06400
1948	06883
1949	07149
1950	07285
1951	07429
1952	07566
1953	07679
1954	07779
1955	07871
1956	07922
1957	07952

APPENDIX IV

Glossary of Terms relating to Paper

Archival Stable over time, resistant to physical change.

Art paper Paper made for artistic processes. Art paper is generally of better quality than commercial paper.

Calendering The process of smoothing the surface of paper with rollers.

Caliper The thickness of a single sheet.

Coated Paper coated with clay or other filler to smooth the surface.

Cold pressed A moderately textured surface produced with cold rollers.

Deckle Part of the frame used to contain the pulp on the surface of the mould. The wavy deckle edge, often called a deckle, is formed when pulp seeps between the deckle and the mould. Handmade paper has four deckle edges; machine made paper has two.

Felt side The top side of the sheet, which is in contact with the felts on the paper-making machine. The felt side is usually smoother than the bottom, or wire side; on most papers, the difference is hardly perceptible.

Filler Clays and minerals added to the pulp to increase the paper's density.

Handmade Paper made by lifting a mould or screen through a tub of pulp by hand.

Grain The direction in which most of the fibers are oriented. Machine-made paper has the grain oriented with the long axis of the machine. Better paper has less grain, and handmade paper has little or no grain.

Hot pressed A smooth paper surface made with hot rollers.

Laid A machine-made texture stamped into the surface of machine made paper. It is designed to loosely emulate the lines left by the screen in hand made paper.

Linter Paper-like sheets of processed wood or cotton designed to be made into pulp. A cotton linter is made from second-grade cotton fiber that is too short for use in textiles.

Mould A flat screen mounted in a frame, on which the pulp is gathered in a tub to form the sheet.

Mouldmade A paper made to emulate a hand made sheet, but made by a machine.

pH A measure of acidity and alkalinity, with seven being neutral, values above seven being alkaline, and values below seven being acid. A pH of 6.5 through 7.5 is considered neutral in paper making.

Pulp The paper fiber, mixed with water.

Rag Traditionally, this term referred to paper made from cotton and linen textiles, as opposed to that made from linters. Textiles are made from the hard, long fiber of the cotton plant, while linters are made from shorter fibers. The term *rag* is increasingly being used to refer to any paper with cotton or linen content, regardless of the source.

Rice paper Lightweight oriental paper. While rice *straw* is sometimes included with other fibers, paper is never made from rice itself.

Rough A relatively textured surface, revealing the sheet as it was produced by the paper making machine.

Size A sealant used to make the paper surface less absorbent. Internal sizing is added to the pulp. Surface sizing is applied after the paper is formed. Tub sizing is applied after the sheet is dried. Beater sizing and engine sizing are terms used for internal sizing.

Sulfate process (sometimes spelled *sulphate*). An alkaline method of reducing wood fibers using sodium sulfate, sodium sulfide, and caustic soda (sodium hydroxide). This process is now the most widely used and produces so-called acid-free paper. The fibers are beaten after reduction.

Sulfite process (sometimes spelled *sulphite*). An acid method of reducing wood fibers, using sodium sulphite.

Watermark A design woven in the wire of the mould, and visible in a sheet of hand made paper. Watermarks are often stamped into machine-made papers.

Wire side See: felt side.

APPENDIX V

Glossary of Terms relating to Printing

Automatic A press which feeds paper automatically, as opposed to a hand-fed press.

Bales See "tympan bales."

Bed The part of the press on which the form is placed. On a platen press, the bed is vertical. On a cylinder press, the bed is usually horizontal.

Bearing rail The surfaces on either side of a cylinder press bed that make contact with the cylinder bearers.

Bearers Heavy, type-high material placed in a form to absorb and even the force of the impression. See also: "roller bearers."

Block Generic term for a plate used to print a graphic, especially when the graphic is a woodcut or linoleum cut. Also, a block of assembled type.

Broadside A poster.

Chase A rectangular steel frame for holding the form on the press. A chase is always used on a platen press, and is sometimes used on a cylinder press.

Composing stick A small three-sided tray held in the hand while setting or composing type. Sticks are now made of steel, but were once made of wood.

Composition Type that is set into words, whether by hand or machine.

Compositor A person who sets (or *composes*) type.

Copy The text from which type is composed or set.

Counter An area of white within a letter form, traditionally formed by driving an appropriately-shaped punch, called a counter punch, into the primary punch used to form the mat. The counter of an 'o,' for example, is the center of the 'o.'

Cut A generic term for a plate that is used to print a photograph or graphic.

Cylinder bearers On a cylinder press, the smooth flanges on each side of the cylinder that contact the bearing rails on the bed.

Dead bar A rectangular bar that lies on a cylinder press bed to prevent type from being placed where the grippers will strike them. Also called a "register bar."

Deadline A line, usually on a cylinder press bed, which shows the boundary of the area in which paper grippers or other parts of the machine will strike and damage the type when the press is operated.

Deboss See: embossing.

Didot The measure used for the height pointwise of type in Continental Europe, which differs slightly from the American point system. The two systems use points of different sizes. See: point.

Display type Type larger than 14 point. Type 14 points and smaller is called *text type*.

Distribute To place type back into the case after printing.

Distributor A roller used to hold and disburse ink to the form rollers, ink disk, or ink table on a press. When in contact with the form rollers, distributor rollers are usually metal, and are shifted from one side of the press to the other by flange running in a worm-like pattern on their shafts. When mounted on an ink disk or table, distributor rollers are usually positioned at an angle to the press and move longitudinally as they rotate. Vandercook called their distributors *vibrators*.

Drawsheet See: "tympan."

Dwell On a powered platen press, the time during which the platen is held stationary for feeding paper. Impression dwell is the time during which the platen is in contact with the form.

Edition A printing, especially the continuous printing of a work that has been developed to its final form. Also, a printing from a setting of type. If type is reprinted, it is a reprinting. If type is reset, it is a new edition.

Em A measure unique to printing which varies with the size of type being measured. An em is the same length as the type's height pointwise, thus an em of 18 point is 18 points. The term is based on the size of an 'M' sort, which is usually cast on a square body of type. The term is used in reference to spaces within the text, and the em is divided into 3-to-the-em, 4-to-the-em, etc., and *multiplied* to make em quads, two em quads, etc. The em was formerly used to measure large amounts of type or the length of lines, but these are now measured in picas.

Embossing A mechanical process that creates a three-dimensional image in a paper's surface, often using two metal or polymer embossing dies, lots of pressure, and heat. Some printers distinguish between embossing (raising the paper surface) and debossing (depressing the surface, as with type).

En A measure, unique to printing, which varies with the size of type being measured. An en equals half the length of the type's height pointwise, thus an en of 18 point is 9 points. The term is only used in reference to a space. It is based on the dimensions of an 'N' sort, which is usually cast on a half-square body of type.

End guides Guides on a cylinder press, usually located between the grippers, that either hold off or cock the leading edge of a sheet. Not all presses are equipped with these.

Engrave To cut with a fine tool. Wood, copper, steel, plastic and stone have been engraved for printing.

Etch To reduce by acid. In relief printing, etching is often used to remove areas of a plate so that they will not print. In intaglio, etching is used to form the incisions that will hold the ink and print. In both cases, a resist that is impermeable to the etching solution (usually an acid) protects the parts of the plate's surface that are to be left intact.

Even measure Lengths which correspond to the common lengths in which furniture is made, including 10, 15, 20, 25, 30, 35 picas, etc. Applied mainly to line lengths.

Face A type design, sometimes called a typeface. Also, the printing surface of a piece of type, a plate, or other surface.

Feed board A table from which the paper stock is fed to a press

Fore-edge The edge of a book opposite the spine when the book is closed. The fore-edge margins are the margins at the right and left edges when the book lies open.

Form The entire body of type, cuts, furniture, rule, etc., mounted or to be mounted on a press. The word is sometimes used to refer to the printing surface within a form.

Form roller A roller on a press that contacts the form.

Font Type of one face and size. A *wrong font* is an individual type which is accidentally mixed with another font, either of another size, or face, or style, as a roman which is mixed in with the italic. The meaning of the term *font* in letterpress is different from that in current, general use, where the term has come to mean *face*.

Foundry type Type cast from hard metal, on machines designed for the additional pressure and heat required. Foundry type must be set by hand, and, because of its cost, is distributed back into cases when the printing is completed.

Flywheel A heavy wheel whose momentum smoothes the movement of a foot-powered or motor-powered press.

Frisket A sheet, usually of paper, used to mask a form on a press and prevent extraneous marks from appearing on the sheet from furniture, bearers, etc.

Furniture Large spacing material, traditionally of wood, but also made in metal and plastic. Furniture is used to fill the blank areas of a form.

Galley A tray used to hold and store type, usually of steel or brass.

Gathering A unit of pages for a book, usually made from a single sheet that is folded to make one of the book's many sections. A gathering is similar to a signature, except that a signature is signed, or marked with a letter of number showing the order in which it should be compiled to form the book.

Gauge pin On a platen press, a small metal device to which the paper is fed. The gauge pins are usually used in sets of three. A long flat pin is stabbed into the tympan when the pins are set, holding the pins in position.

Gripper On a platen press, a gripper is heavy metal tongue which swings into position to hold the paper against the tympan as the press closes; they are usually used in pairs. On a cylinder press, the grippers are clamps that hold the paper on the cylinder at the paper's leading edge.

Gutter The margins nearest the binding in a book. In a conventional book layout, the gutter lies between the two blocks of text on facing pages.

Hand A prefix meaning powered or done by hand. Thus: *hand cylinder press, hand-fed press.* A *hand press,* however, is a particular kind of press, with a platen that is lowered by lever action onto a horizontal bed.

Hand-set type Type picked from cases and placed in a stick by hand.

Head On a cylinder press, the side of the bed which first meets the cylinder during the impression. On a hand press, the side of a bed nearest the frame when the bed is run out. Traditionally, the head or top of the form is placed at head of the press. In a book, or a form used to print a book, the head is the top, or the edge which is farthest from the reader when the book is used.

Ink disk On a platen press, the round steel surface serves as a reservoir for ink, typically at the top of the press.

Intaglio A printing process that uses lines etched or engraved below the surface of the plate to hold ink.

Kerning An adjustment in letterspacing that brings two letters closer together. With letterpress type, kerning is usually done by cutting *kerns* in the type bodies so that they mate; type can also be cast with a kern.

Lead (noun) Spacing material made of typemetal that is two points in depth. A one point lead is also made, but is less common. Pronounced like the metal.

Lead (verb) To insert spacing, usually two point leads, between lines. Leading is a way to make text appear less congested on the page. Pronounced like the metal.

Letter spacing The space between letters.

Letterpress The process and equipment used to print text from type.

Line A measure used with wood type, with one line equal to one pica. See also "rule."

Line length The length of a line of type, usually measured in picas.

Line spacing The space between lines of type.

Linotype Both a casting machine and the matter that it makes. Linotype composition is made of entire lines of letters cast as a unit, one line at a time, from a row of mats arranged by keyboard.

Lithography A printing process that relies on the chemical separation of water and ink on a smooth plate.

Lock up The process of preparing a form for mounting on a press by applying pressure with quoins.

Machine composition Typesetting which is done without picking type from cases by hand. The two most common kinds of machine composition are Linotype and Monotype.

Machine platen A platen press that runs continuously, either with an electric motor or a treadle. Machine platens are typically equipped with flywheels.

Makeready The process of preparing a press to print by adjusting the pressure exerted on the paper and type or plate, especially when underlays and overlays are used. The term is sometimes used to include all preparations, including lubrication, inking, and paper feeding adjustments.

Manuscript A paper copy of writing intended to be set into type.

Mat A metal surface with a character cut or etched into it, used to cast type. A *mat* is the same as a *matrix*.

Matrix A mat. The plural of *matrix* is *matrices*.

Material Cast rule and spacing material.

Matter Anything that is printed from in letterpress.

Monotype Both a typecasting machine and the type that it produces. Monotype is much like foundry type, though it is usually made of metal which is softer than foundry metal.

Monotype composition See: Machine composition.

Numbering machine A small machine for printing numbers which automatically advances with each impression. A numbering machine can be included in any ordinary letterpress form.

Offset The transfer of ink from one surface to another. The term refers to a method used by wood engravers and others to transfer the image of one block to another on a press. In commercial lithography, *offset* refers to the transfer of ink from the lithographic plate to a rubber blanket. The blanket then transfers the ink to the sheet. In letterpress, the term refers to the accidental transfer from the printed surface of one sheet to the back of its neighbor in a stack of freshly-printed sheets, more properly called set-off.

Overlay Paper or other material placed in the packing or on the tympan to increase impression.

Packing Hard paper or card stock used to pad the platen or cylinder surface. Packing is placed under the tympan.

Perfecting press A press that prints on both sides of the paper.

Photopolymer A plastic that is changed from water soluble to water resistant with exposure to ultra-violet light. Flat plates are used for relief printing.

Photoengraving A process of converting a photographic or other image into a relief plate with the use of photo-sensitive resists and mordants that erode the surface. Also, the plate itself.

Pica A unit of measure unique to printing and applied to spacing material and general measurement. A pica is about ³⁄₁₆ of an inch and is quite close to 4 mm. Twelve points make one pica.

Pie, pied type Type which has fallen into a confused jumble. Pie, pronounced like the food, is both a verb (don't pie the type!) and a noun (let's move this pie). Pie is the same as pied type.

Platen A heavy casting with a flat surface against which the impression is made on a platen press or hand press. The paper is positioned between the platen and the form, and the platen and form meet to make the impression.

Point A measure of paper thickness for heavy stock, in which one point equals .0001 inch. Also, a unit of measure unique to printing and applied only to type and a few spacing materials. The American point system was adopted in 1886, with a point equal to .3514 mm., or .01383″. There are approximately 72 points to the inch. The English point is said to be .00005 mm larger. Twelve points is a common size for text type. In the Didot system used in Continental Europe, a point equals .35 mm.

Printer A human who operates a printing press. The term is never applied to a press.

Quoin A small expandable device used to develop pressure or force within a chase or on a bed; the pressure holds the many individual pieces of the form together. Originally, quoins were simply wedges. Quoins are operated with a quoin key.

Register The position of printed matter on stock. The word is also used as a verb, meaning to coordinate the position of the printing and the margins, or the printing and something previously printed.

Register See: Dead bar.

Reglet Thin spacing material made of wood and measuring one half or one pica in thickness. They are usually kept in cabinets, in increments of 5 and 10 picas in length. A thin reglet is half a pica (6 points) thick, while a reglet is a pica (12 points) thick.

Relief The process of printing from a raised surface that is inked and pressed into paper.

Roller bearers Wide strips of type-high material placed in a form to prevent the ink roller from slurring and from wiping the type clean, rather than inking it. The roller bearers are placed so that they print outside of the sheet.

Roller saddle The cradle for the roller shafts, which holds the rollers on a platen press.

Roller trucks Wheels mounted on the roller shafts which rotate the rollers and hold them at the proper height above the form. Roller trucks are usually found on platen presses.

Rotary press A press with the printing type or plate mounted on the surface of a cylinder.

Rule A wood or metal surface designed to print as a line or a linear pattern. Rule is made in many sizes, from hairline to many picas in width.

Serif A serif is a small perpendicular line that terminates the linear strokes of a letter.

Set-off The accidental transfer from the printed surface of one sheet to the back of its neighbor in a stack of freshly-printed sheets, sometimes called offset.

Set width The width of a sort, measured line-wise.

Sheet A single piece of paper. The word is often used to refer to paper cut and ready for a particular printing project.

Sheet fingers On a cylinder press, the metal fingers that apply light pressure to the sheet and hold it against the cylinder as the cylinder rotates. See also: "sheet rollers."

Sheet rollers Vandercook's term for sheet fingers. Challenge called them both "sheet fingers" and "stripper fingers."

Side arm A linkage which connects the bed and the wheels at the front of a platen press.

Signature See: "gathering"

Slug Spacing material made of typemetal that is half a pica in thickness.

Sort An individual piece of type.

Stock Paper which is intended for printing, especially the actual paper that is cut and ready for a particular printing project.

Stone A flat surface, usually of marble or steel, which is used to prepare type for mounting on a press.

Stonework The work done to prepare a form for printing, including surrounding it with furniture and locking it up. The term derives from the use of stone, usually marble, as a working surface.

Straight matter Continuous text, as distinct from headlines, display lines, running heads, etc.

Stripper fingers See: sheet fingers.

Quoins Wedges and other devices which expand to apply pressure to a form and keep its parts rigidly in place.

Tail The side opposite the head. See "head."

Take-off board A table onto which the printed stock is placed.

Text type Type smaller than 18 point. Type 18 points and larger is called "display type."

Thin space A narrow space made of brass or copper.

Throw-off A mechanism for separating the bed and platen, or the bed and cylinder, so that no impression is made. On platen presses, a throw-off is only fitted on a foot or motor powered press. On small cylinder presses, the throw-off is sometimes called a *trip*.

Trip See: throw-off.

Tympan The outer layer of paper covering the platen or cylinder. The tympan is sometimes called a *drawsheet*.

Tympan bales Metal clamps which secure the tympan to the platen.

Tympan packing See "packing."

Type Letters made in wood or metal. The term usually refers to material collectively that is made of individual pieces, that is, with one letter on its own piece of type, rather than to Linotype material. The word also refers to individual pieces of type, or sorts, as: "I dropped a type."

Type block See: "block."

Typeface See: "face."

Type high The height of type (from the base to printing surface). Type high equals .918 inches in the U.S., Canada, and England.

Type metal A combination of lead, tin, and antimony that is used in varying combinations to cast type.

Underlay Paper or other material placed under type to increase impression.

Vibrator See: "distributor."

Wheels On a platen press, the round castings on each side that transfer the motion of the main shaft and its gear train to the side arms, which in turn give movement to the bed.

White space Unprinted areas on a printed sheet.

Woodcut A block which is cut and carved with steel tools on the surface of the side-grain. Also, a print made from such a block. The woodcut yields crude, bold lines.

Wood engraving A block which is cut and carved with steel tools on the surface of the end-grain. Also, a print made from such a block. The wood engraving yields fine, precise lines.

Word spacing The space between words.

Checklist for moving equipment

For any move, the following are essential things to have along:
- work gloves
- work clothes that can be sullied with dirt and grease
- tools, including an oil can
- tape measure
- machinery (or rigger's) casters, or a machine dolly, or rollers, or a pallet jack
- jacks, or a Johnson bar, or some kind of lifting equipment
- heavy straps or chain for moving and securing the load
- rope
- moving blankets
- blocks
- small dollies or platform trucks
- rags
- hand cleaner (diaper wipes work well)
- tire gauge
- heavy broom and dustpan
- plenty of help

Check tire pressure on trailers and trucks before setting out on moving day.

The following are optional:
- knee pads
- cardboard cut to galley and/or case size
- plastic wrap
- hammer and nails, 2 × 4s, crowbar
- tarps
- air compressor and blowgun at home

Checklist for closing shop

A checklist for closing ones shop at the end of a session can be useful so that basic housekeeping functions aren't forgotten. Mine looks like this:
- Presses cleaned
- Rollers clear of contact
- Ink cans closed
- Ink knives and surfaces cleaned
- Power to press controls off
- Rags laid out or placed in fireproof containers

200

INDEX

LETTERPRESS PRINTING
was composed in digital versions of
three classic American typefaces of the letterpress era.

MONTICELLO is based on one of the earliest American typefaces, Binny & Ronaldson's Roman #1, cut in Philadelphia in the late eighteenth century. The face was cut for hot-metal Linotype composition in 1946 when Princeton University Press began publishing the papers of president Thomas Jefferson, who had been a helpful supporter of the Binny & Ronaldson foundry. More recently the face has been revived for computer composition as Princeton continued its Jefferson papers program. The computer version was made by Matthew Carter.

FRANKLIN GOTHIC CONDENSED is a member of an extensive family originally designed early in the twentieth century by Morris Fuller Benton for the American Typefounders Company. The version made for computer composition was designed in the late 1900s by Victor Caruso and David Berlow for the International Typeface Corporation.

Morris Fuller Benton also was responsible for the design of CLOISTER OPEN FACE for the American Typefounders Company about 1929. It is among many types based on the fifteenth-century Venetian typefaces of Nicolas Jenson.

Page design & composition were done by
Will Powers, Birchwood, Minnesota.

Letterpress Printing was printed lithographically by
Sheridan Books, Ann Arbor, Michigan.